New York Mets 2021

A Baseball Companion

Edited by Steven Goldman and Bret Sayre

Baseball Prospectus

Craig Brown, Associate Editor
Robert Au, Harry Pavlidis and Amy Pircher, Statistics Editors

Copyright © 2021 by DIY Baseball, LLC.
All rights reserved

This book or any part thereof may not be reproduced or transmitted in any form or by any means, electronic or mechanical, including photocopying, recording, or by any information storage and retrieval system, without permission in writing from the publisher.

Limit of Liability/Disclaimer of Warranty: While the publisher and the author have used their best efforts in preparing this book, they make no representations or warranties with respect to the accuracy or completeness of the contents of this book and specifically disclaim any implied warranties of merchantability or fitness for a particular purpose. No warranty may be created or extended by sales representatives or written sales materials. The advice and strategies contained herein may not be suitable for your situation. You should consult with a professional where appropriate. Neither the publisher nor the author shall be liable for any loss of profit or any other commercial damages, including but not limited to special, incidental, consequential, or other damages.

Library of Congress Cataloging-in-Publication Data:
paperback
ISBN-13: 978-1-950716-59-3

Project Credits
Cover Design: Ginny Searle
Interior Design and Production: Amy Pircher, Robert Au
Layout: Amy Pircher, Robert Au

Baseball icon courtesy of Uberux, from https://www.shareicon.net/author/uberux

Ballpark diagram courtesy of Lou Spirito/THIRTY81 Project, https://thirty81project.com/

Manufactured in the United States of America
10 9 8 7 6 5 4 3 2 1

Table of Contents

Statistical Introduction v

Part 1: Team Analysis
Performance Graphs 3
2020 Team Performance 4
2021 Team Projections 5
Team Personnel 8
Citi Field Stats 9
Mets Team Analysis 11

Part 2: Player Analysis
Mets Player Analysis 18
Mets Prospects 113

Part 3: Featured Articles
Mets All-Time Top 10 Players 125
    by Rob Mains

A Taxonomy of 2020 Abnormalities 131
    by Rob Mains

Tranches of WAR 137
    by Russell A. Carleton

Secondhand Sport 143
    by Patrick Dubuque

Steve Dalkowski Dreaming 147
    by Steven Goldman

A Reward For A Functioning Society 151
    by Cory Frontin and Craig Goldstein

Index of Names 155

Statistical Introduction

Sports are, fundamentally, a blend of athletic endeavor and storytelling. Baseball, like any other sport, tells its stories in so many ways: in the arc of a game from the stands or a season from the box scores, in photos, or even in numbers. At Baseball Prospectus, we understand that statistics don't replace observation or any of baseball's stories, but complement everything else that makes the game so much fun.

What stats help us with is with patterns and precision, variance and value. This book can help you learn things you may not see from watching a game or hundred, whether it's the path of a career over time or the breadth of the entire MLB. We'd also never ask you to choose between our numbers and the experience of viewing a game from the cheap seats or the comfort of your home; our publication combines running the numbers with observations and wisdom from some of the brightest minds we can find. But if you *do* want to learn more about the numbers beyond what's on the backs of player jerseys, let us help explain.

Offense

We've revised our methodology for determining batting value. Long-time readers of the book will notice that we've retired True Average in favor of a new metric: Deserved Runs Created Plus (DRC+). Developed by Jonathan Judge and our stats team, this statistic measures everything a player does at the plate–reaching base, hitting for power, making outs, and moving runners over–and puts it on a scale where 100 equals league-average performance. A DRC+ of 150 is terrific, a DRC+ of 100 is average and a DRC+ of 75 means you better be an excellent defender.

DRC+ also does a better job than any of our previous metrics in taking contextual factors into account. The model adjusts for how the park affects performance, but also for things like the talent of the opposing pitcher, value of different types of batted-ball events, league, temperature and other factors. It's able to describe a player's expected offensive contribution than any other statistic we've found over the years, and also does a better job of predicting future performance as well.

The other aspect of run-scoring is baserunning, which we quantify using Baserunning Runs. BRR not only records the value of stolen bases (or getting caught in the act), but also accounts for all the stuff that doesn't show up on the back of a baseball card: a runner's ability to go first to third on a single, or advance on a fly ball.

Defense

Where offensive value is *relatively* easy to identify and understand, defensive value is ... not. Over the past dozen years, the sabermetric community has focused mostly on stats based on zone data: a real-live human person records the type of batted ball and estimated landing location, and models are created that give expected outs. From there, you can compare fielders' actual outs to those expected ones. Simple, right?

Unfortunately, zone data has two major issues. First, zone data is recorded by commercial data providers who keep the raw data private unless you pay for it. (All the statistics we build in this book and on our website use public data as inputs.) That hurts our ability to test assumptions or duplicate results. Second, over the years it has become apparent that there's quite a bit of "noise" in zone-based fielding analysis. Sometimes the conclusions drawn from zone data don't hold up to scrutiny, and sometimes the different data provided by different providers don't look anything alike, giving wildly different results. Sometimes the hard-working professional stringers or scorers might unknowingly inflict unconscious bias into the mix: for example good fielders will often be credited with more expected outs despite the data, and ballparks with high press boxes tend to score more line drives than ones with a lower press box.

Enter our Fielding Runs Above Average (FRAA). For most positions, FRAA is built from play-by-play data, which allows us to avoid the subjectivity found in many other fielding metrics. The idea is this: count how many fielding plays are made by a given player and compare that to expected plays for an average fielder at their position (based on pitcher ground ball tendencies and batter handedness). Then we adjust for park and base-out situations.

When it comes to catchers, our methodology is a little different thanks to the laundry list of responsibilities they're tasked with beyond just, well, catching and throwing the ball. By now you've probably heard about "framing" or the art of making umpires more likely to call balls outside the strike zone for strikes. To put this into one tidy number, we incorporate pitch tracking data (for the years it exists) and adjust for important factors like pitcher, umpire, batter and home-field advantage using a mixed-model approach. This grants us a number for how many strikes the catcher is personally adding to (or subtracting from) his pitchers' performance ... which we then convert to runs added or lost using linear weights.

Framing is one of the biggest parts of determining catcher value, but we also take into account blocking balls from going past, whether a scorer deems it a passed ball or a wild pitch. We use a similar approach—one that really benefits from the pitch tracking data that tells us what ends up in the dirt and what doesn't. We also include a catcher's ability to prevent stolen bases and how well they field balls in play, and *finally* we come up with our FRAA for catchers.

Pitching

Both pitching and fielding make up the half of baseball that isn't run scoring: run prevention. Separating pitching from fielding is a tough task, and most recent pitching analysis has branched off from Voros McCracken's famous (and controversial) statement, "There is little if any difference among major-league pitchers in their ability to prevent hits on balls hit in the field of play." The research of the analytic community has validated this to some extent, and there are a host of "defense-independent" pitching measures that have been developed to try and extract the effect of the defense behind a hurler from the pitcher's work.

Our solution to this quandary is Deserved Run Average (DRA), our core pitching metric. DRA seeks to evaluate a pitcher's performance, much like earned run average (ERA), the tried-and-true pitching stat you've seen on every baseball broadcast or box score from the past century, but it's very different. To start, DRA takes an event-by-event look at what the pitchers does, and adjusts the value of that event based on different environmental factors like park, batter, catcher, umpire, base-out situation, run differential, inning, defense, home field advantage, pitcher role and temperature. That mixed model gives us a pitcher's expected contribution, similar to what we do for our DRC+ model for hitters and FRAA model for catchers. (Oh, and we also consider the pitcher's effect on basestealing and on balls getting past the catcher.)

DRA is set to the scale of runs allowed per nine innings (RA9) instead of ERA, which makes DRA's scale slightly higher than ERA's. Because of this, for ease of use, we're supplying DRA-, which is much easier for the reader to parse. As with DRC+, DRA- is an "index" stat, meaning instead of using some arbitrary and shifting number to denote what's "good," average is always 100. The reason that it uses a minus rather than a plus is because like ERA, a lower number is better. Therefore a 75 DRA- describes a performance 25 percent better than average, whereas a 150 DRA- means that either a pitcher is getting extremely lucky with their results, or getting ready to try a new pitch.

Since the last time you picked up an edition of this book, we've also made a few minor changes to DRA to make it better. Recent research into "tunneling"—the act of throwing consecutive pitches that appear similar from a batter's point of view until after the swing decision point–data has given us a new contextual factor to account for in DRA: plate distance. This refers to the distance between successive pitches as they approach the plate, and while it has a smaller effect than factors like velocity or whiff rate, it still can help explain pitcher strikeout rate in our model.

Recently Added Descriptive Statistics

Returning to our 2021 edition of the book are a few figures which recently appeared. These numbers may be a little bit more familiar to those of you who have spent some time investigating baseball statistics.

Fastball Percentage

Our fastball percentage (FA%) statistic measures how frequently a pitcher throws a pitch classified as a "fastball," measured as a percentage of overall pitches thrown. We qualify three types of fastballs:

1. The traditional four-seam fastball;
2. The two-seam fastball or sinker;
3. "Hard cutters," which are pitches that have the movement profile of a cut fastball and are used as the pitcher's primary offering or in place of a more traditional fastball.

For example, a pitcher with a FA% of 67 throws any combination of these three pitches about two-thirds of the time.

Whiff Rate

Everybody loves a swing and a miss, and whiff rate (Whiff%) measures how frequently pitchers induce a swinging strike. To calculate Whiff%, we add up all the pitches thrown that ended with a swinging strike, then divide that number by a pitcher's total pitches thrown. Most often, high whiff rates correlate with high strikeout rates (and overall effective pitcher performance).

Called Strike Probability

Called Strike Probability (CSP) is a number that represents the likelihood that all of a pitcher's pitches will be called a strike while controlling for location, pitcher and batter handedness, umpire and count. Here's how it works: on each pitch, our model determines how many times (out of 100) that a similar pitch was called for a strike given those factors mentioned above, and when normalized for each batter's strike zone. Then we average the CSP for all pitches thrown by a pitcher in a season, and that gives us the yearly CSP percentage you see in the stats boxes.

As you might imagine, pitchers with a higher CSP are more likely to work in the zone, where pitchers with a lower CSP are likely locating their pitches outside the normal strike zone, for better or for worse.

Projections

Many of you aren't turning to this book just for a look at what a player has done, but for a look at what a player is going to do: the PECOTA projections. PECOTA, initially developed by Nate Silver (who has moved on to greater fame as a political analyst), consists of three parts:

1. Major-league equivalencies, which use minor-league statistics to project how a player will perform in the major leagues;
2. Baseline forecasts, which use weighted averages and regression to the mean to estimate a player's current true talent level; and
3. Aging curves, which uses the career paths of comparable players to estimate how a player's statistics are likely to change over time.

With all those important things covered, let's take a look at what's in the book this year.

Team Prospectus

Most of this book is composed of team chapters, with one for each of the 30 major-league franchises. On the first page of each chapter, you'll see a box that contains some of the key statistics for each team as well as a very inviting stadium diagram.

We start with the team name, their unadjusted 2020 win-loss record, and their divisional ranking. Beneath that are a host of other team statistics. **Pythag** presents an adjusted 2020 winning percentage, calculated by taking runs scored per game (**RS/G**) and runs allowed per game (**RA/G**) for the team, and running them through a version of Bill James' Pythagorean formula that was refined and improved by David Smyth and Brandon Heipp. (The formula is called "Pythagenpat," which is equally fun to type and to say.)

Next up is **DRC+**, described earlier, to indicate the overall hitting ability of the team either above or below league-average. Run prevention on the pitching side is covered by **DRA** (also mentioned earlier) and another metric: Fielding Independent Pitching (**FIP**), which calculates another ERA-like statistic based on strikeouts, walks, and home runs recorded. Defensive Efficiency Rating (**DER**) tells us the percentage of balls in play turned into outs for the team, and is a quick fielding shorthand that rounds out run prevention.

After that, we have several measures related to roster composition, as opposed to on-field performance. **B-Age** and **P-Age** tell us the average age of a team's batters and pitchers, respectively. **Payroll** is the combined team payroll for all on-field players, and Doug Pappas' Marginal Dollars per Marginal Win (**M$/MW**) tells us how much money a team spent to earn production above replacement level.

Next to each of these stats, we've listed each team's MLB rank in that category from first to 30th. In this, first always indicates a positive outcome and 30th a negative outcome, except in the case of salary—first is highest.

After the franchise statistics, we share a few items about the team's home ballpark. There's the aforementioned diagram of the park's dimensions (including distances to the outfield wall), a graphic showing the height of the wall from the left-field pole to the right-field pole, and a table showing three-year park factors for the stadium. The park factors are displayed as indexes where 100 is average, 110 means that the park inflates the statistic in question by 10 percent, and 90 means that the park deflates the statistic in question by 10 percent.

On the second page of each team chapter, you'll find three graphs. The first is **Payroll History** and helps you see how the team's payroll has compared to the MLB and divisional average payrolls over time. Payroll figures are current as of January 1, 2021; with so many free agents still unsigned as of this writing, the final 2021 figure will likely be significantly different for many teams. (In the meantime, you can always find the most current data at Baseball Prospectus' Cot's Baseball Contracts page.)

The second graph is **Future Commitments** and helps you see the team's future outlays, if any.

The third graph is **Farm System Ranking** and displays how the Baseball Prospectus prospect team has ranked the organization's farm system since 2007.

After the graphs, we have a **Personnel** section that lists many of the important decision-makers and upper-level field and operations staff members for the franchise, as well as any former Baseball Prospectus staff members who are currently part of the organization. (In very rare circumstances, someone might be on both lists!)

Position Players

After all that information and a thoughtful bylined essay covering each team, we present our player comments. These are also bylined, but due to frequent franchise shifts during the offseason, our bylines are more a rough guide than a perfect accounting of who wrote what.

Each player is listed with the major-league team that employed him as of early January 2021. If a player changed teams after that point via free agency, trade, or any other method, you'll be able to find them in the chapter for their previous squad.

As an example, take a look at the player comment for Padres shortstop Fernando Tatis Jr.: the stat block that accompanies his written comment is at the top of this page. First we cover biographical information (age is as of June 30, 2021) before moving onto the stats themselves. Our statistic columns include standard identifying information like **YEAR**, **TEAM**, **LVL** (level of affiliated play) and **AGE** before getting into the numbers. Next, we provide raw, untranslated

www.baseballprospectus.com

Fernando Tatis Jr. SS
Born: 01/02/99   Age: 22   Bats: R   Throws: R
Height: 6'3"   Weight: 217   Origin: International Free Agent, 2015

YEAR	TEAM	LVL	AGE	PA	R	2B	3B	HR	RBI	BB	K	SB	CS	AVG/OBP/SLG
2018	SA	AA	19	394	77	22	4	16	43	33	109	16	5	.286/.355/.507
2019	SD	MLB	20	372	61	13	6	22	53	30	110	16	6	.317/.379/.590
2020	SD	MLB	21	257	50	11	2	17	45	27	61	11	3	.277/.366/.571
2021 FS	SD	MLB	22	600	95	24	4	31	81	50	165	17	8	.263/.331/.499
2021 DC	SD	MLB	22	628	100	25	4	32	85	53	173	19	8	.263/.331/.499

Comparables: Darryl Strawberry, Bo Bichette, Ronald Acuña Jr.

YEAR	TEAM	LVL	AGE	PA	DRC+	BABIP	BRR	FRAA	WARP
2018	SA	AA	19	394	136	.370	3.0	SS(83): -1.9	2.4
2019	SD	MLB	20	372	118	.410	7.1	SS(83): 0.9	3.4
2020	SD	MLB	21	257	126	.306	0.7	SS(57): -5.5	0.9
2021 FS	SD	MLB	22	600	126	.318	1.7	SS -1	3.9
2021 DC	SD	MLB	22	628	126	.318	1.8	SS -1	4.0

numbers like you might find on the back of your dad's baseball cards: **PA** (plate appearances), **R** (runs), **2B** (doubles), **3B** (triples), **HR** (home runs), **RBI** (runs batted in), **BB** (walks), **K** (strikeouts), **SB** (stolen bases) and **CS** (caught stealing).

Following the basic stats is **Whiff%** (whiff rate), which denotes how often, when a batter swings, he fails to make contact with the ball. Another way to think of this number is an inverse of a hitter's contact rate.

Next, we have unadjusted "slash" statistics: **AVG** (batting average), **OBP** (on-base percentage) and **SLG** (slugging percentage). Following the slash line is **DRC+** (Deserved Runs Created Plus), which we described earlier as total offensive expected contribution compared to the league average.

BABIP (batting average on balls in play) tells us how often a ball in play fell for a hit, and can help us identify whether a batter may have been lucky or not ... but note that high BABIPs also tend to follow the great hitters of our time, as well as speedy singles hitters who put the ball on the ground.

The next item is **BRR** (Baserunning Runs), which covers all of a player's baserunning accomplishments including (but not limited to) swiped bags and failed attempts. Next is **FRAA** (Fielding Runs Above Average), which also includes the number of games previously played at each position noted in parentheses. Multi-position players have only their two most frequent positions listed here, but their total FRAA number reflects all positions played.

Our last column here is **WARP** (Wins Above Replacement Player). WARP estimates the total value of a player, which means for hitters it takes into account hitting runs above average (calculated using the DRC+ model), BRR and FRAA. Then, it makes an adjustment for positions played and gives the player a credit for plate appearances based upon the difference between "replacement level"—which is derived from the quality of players added to a team's roster after the start of the season–and the league average.

The final line just below the stats box is **PECOTA** data, which is discussed further in a following section.

Catchers

Catchers are a special breed, and thus they have earned their own separate box which displays some of the defensive metrics that we've built just for them. As an example, let's check out Yasmani Grandal.

YEAR	TEAM	P. COUNT	FRM RUNS	BLK RUNS	THRW RUNS	TOT RUNS
2018	LAD	16816	15.7	0.8	0.1	16.5
2019	MIL	18740	19.4	1.8	-0.1	21.1
2020	CHW	4830	3.7	0.3	-0.2	3.8
2021	CHW	14430	16.7	-0.6	1.0	17.1
2021	CHW	14430	16.7	0.4	1.0	18.0

The **YEAR** and **TEAM** columns match what you'd find in the other stat box. **P. COUNT** indicates the number of pitches thrown while the catcher was behind the plate, including swinging strikes, fouls and balls in play. **FRM RUNS** is the total run value the catcher provided (or cost) his team by influencing the umpire to call strikes where other catchers did not. **BLK RUNS** expresses the total run value above or below average for the catcher's ability to prevent wild pitches and passed balls. **THRW RUNS** is calculated using a similar model as the previous two statistics, and it measures a catcher's ability to throw out basestealers but also to dissuade them from testing his arm in the first place. It takes into account factors like the pitcher (including his delivery and pickoff move) and baserunner (who could be as fast as Billy Hamilton or as slow as Yonder Alonso). **TOT RUNS** is the sum of all of the previous three statistics.

Pitchers

Let's give our pitchers a turn, using 2020 AL Cy Young winner Shane Bieber as our example. Take a look at his stat block: the first line and the **YEAR**, **TEAM**, **LVL** and **AGE** columns are the same as in the position player example earlier.

Here too, we have a series of columns that display raw, unadjusted statistics compiled by the pitcher over the course of a season: **W** (wins), **L** (losses), **SV** (saves), **G** (games pitched), **GS** (games started), **IP** (innings pitched), **H** (hits allowed) and **HR** (home runs allowed). Next we have two statistics that are rates: **BB/9** (walks per nine innings) and **K/9** (strikeouts per nine innings), before returning to the unadjusted K (strikeouts).

Next up is **GB%** (ground ball percentage), which is the percentage of all batted balls that were hit on the ground, including both outs and hits. Remember, this is based on observational data and subject to human error, so please approach this with a healthy dose of skepticism.

BABIP (batting average on balls in play) is calculated using the same methodology as it is for position players, but it often tells us more about a pitcher than it does a hitter. With pitchers, a high BABIP is often due to poor defense or bad luck, and can often be an indicator of potential rebound, and a low BABIP may be cause to expect performance regression. (A typical league-average BABIP is close to .290-.300.)

The metrics **WHIP** (walks plus hits per inning pitched) and **ERA** (earned run average) are old standbys: WHIP measures walks and hits allowed on a per-inning basis, while ERA measures earned runs on a nine-inning basis. Neither of these stats are translated or adjusted.

DRA- (Deserved Run Average) was described at length earlier, and measures how the pitcher "deserved" to perform compared to other pitchers. Please note that since we lack all the data points that would make for a "real" DRA for minor-league events, the DRA- displayed for minor league partial-seasons is based off of different data. (That data is a modified version of our cFIP metric, which you can find more information about on our website.)

Shane Bieber RHP
Born: 05/31/95 Age: 26 Bats: R Throws: R
Height: 6'3" Weight: 200 Origin: Round 4, 2016 Draft (#122 overall)

YEAR	TEAM	LVL	AGE	W	L	SV	G	GS	IP	H	HR	BB/9	K/9	K	GB%	BABIP
2018	AKR	AA	23	3	0	0	5	5	31	26	1	0.3	8.7	30	47.3%	.278
2018	COL	AAA	23	3	1	0	8	8	48[2]	30	3	1.1	8.7	47	52.0%	.227
2018	CLE	MLB	23	11	5	0	20	19	114[2]	130	13	1.8	9.3	118	46.2%	.356
2019	CLE	MLB	24	15	8	0	34	33	214[1]	186	31	1.7	10.9	259	44.4%	.298
2020	CLE	MLB	25	8	1	0	12	12	77[1]	46	7	2.4	14.2	122	48.4%	.267
2021 FS	CLE	MLB	26	10	6	0	26	26	150	121	18	2.1	11.7	195	45.5%	.297
2021 DC	CLE	MLB	26	14	7	0	30	30	196.7	159	24	2.1	11.7	257	45.5%	.297

Comparables: Luis Severino, Danny Salazar, Joe Musgrove

YEAR	TEAM	LVL	AGE	WHIP	ERA	DRA-	WARP	MPH	FB%	WHF	CSP
2018	AKR	AA	23	0.87	1.16	61	0.9				
2018	COL	AAA	23	0.74	1.66	69	1.2				
2018	CLE	MLB	23	1.33	4.55	74	2.6	94.7	57.4%	26.2%	
2019	CLE	MLB	24	1.05	3.28	75	4.9	94.4	45.8%	30.8%	
2020	CLE	MLB	25	0.87	1.63	53	2.6	95.3	53.6%	40.7%	
2021 FS	CLE	MLB	26	1.04	2.44	64	4.4	94.7	50.0%	33.2%	44.2%
2021 DC	CLE	MLB	26	1.04	2.44	64	5.8	94.7	50.0%	33.2%	44.2%

Just like with hitters, **WARP** (Wins Above Replacement Player) is a total value metric that puts pitchers of all stripes on the same scale as position players. We use DRA as the primary input for our calculation of WARP. You might notice that relief pitchers (due to their limited innings) may have a lower WARP than you were expecting or than you might see in other WARP-like metrics. WARP does not take leverage into account, just the actions a pitcher performs and the expected value of those actions ... which ends up judging high-leverage relief pitchers differently than you might imagine given their prestige and market value.

MPH gives you the pitcher's 95th percentile velocity for the noted season, in order to give you an idea of what the *peak* fastball velocity a pitcher possesses. Since this comes from our pitch-tracking data, it is not publicly available for minor-league pitchers.

Finally, we display the three new pitching metrics we described earlier. **FB%** (fastball percentage) gives you the percentage of fastballs thrown out of all pitches. **WHF** (whiff rate) tells you the percentage of swinging strikes induced out of all pitches. **CSP** (called strike probability) expresses the likelihood of all pitches thrown to result in a called strike, after controlling for factors like handedness, umpire, pitch type, count and location.

PECOTA

All players have PECOTA projections for 2021, as well as a set of other numbers that describe the performance of comparable players according to PECOTA. All projections for 2021 are for the player at the date we went to press in early January and are projected into the league and park context as indicated by the team abbreviation. (Note that players at very low levels of the minors are too unpredictable to assess using these numbers.) All PECOTA projected statistics represent a player's projected major-league performance.

How we're doing that is a little different this season. There are really two different values that go into the final stat line that you see for PECOTA: How a player performs, and how much playing time he'll be given to perform it. In the past we've estimated playing time based on each team's roster and depth charts, and we'll continue to do that. These projections are denoted as **2021 DC**.

But in many cases, a player won't be projected for major-league playing time; most of the time this is because they aren't projected to be major-league players at all, but still developing as prospects. Or perhaps a player will provide Triple-A depth, only to have an opportunity open up because of injury. For these purposes, we're also supplying a second projection, labeled **2021 FS**, or full season. This is what we would project the player to provide in 600 plate appearances or 150 innings pitched.

Below the projections are the player's three highest-scoring comparable players as determined by PECOTA. All comparables represent a snapshot of how the listed player was performing at the same age as the current player, so if a

23-year-old pitcher is compared to Bartolo Colón, he's actually being compared to a 23-year-old Colón, not the version that pitched for the Rangers in 2018, nor to Colón's career as a whole.

A few points about pitcher projections. First, we aren't yet projecting peak velocity, so that column will be blank in the PECOTA lines. Second, projecting DRA is trickier than evaluating past performance, because it is unclear how deserving each pitcher will be of his anticipated outcomes. However, we know that another DRA-related statistic–contextual FIP or cFIP–estimates future run scoring very well. So for PECOTA, the projected DRA- figures you see are based on the past cFIPs generated by the pitcher and comparable players over time, along with the other factors described above.

If you're familiar with PECOTA, then you'll have noticed that the projection system often appears bullish on players coming off a bad year and bearish on players coming off a good year. (This is because the system weights several previous seasons, not just the most recent one.) In addition, we publish the 50th percentile projections for each player–which is smack in the middle of the range of projected production—which tends to mean PECOTA stat lines don't often have extreme results like 40 home runs or 250 strikeouts in a given season. In essence, PECOTA doesn't project very many extreme seasons.

Managers

After all those wonderful team chapters, we've got statistics for each big-league manager, all of whom are organized by alphabetical order. Here you'll find a block including an extraordinary amount of information collected from each manager's entire career. For more information on the acronyms and what they mean, please visit the Glossary at www.baseballprospectus.com.

There is one important metric that we'd like to call attention to, and you'll find it next to each manager's name: **wRM+** (weighted reliever management plus). Developed by Rob Arthur and Rian Watt, wRM+ investigates how good a manager is at using their best relievers during the moments of highest leverage, using both our proprietary DRA metric as well as Leverage Index. wRM+ is scaled to a league average of 100, and a wRM+ of 105 indicates that relievers were used approximately five percent "better" than average. On the other hand, a wRM+ of 95 would tell us the team used its relievers five percent "worse" than the average team.

While wRM+ does not have an extremely strong correlation with a manager, it is statistically significant; this means that a manager is not *entirely* responsible for a team's wRM+, but does have some effect on that number.

Part 1: Team Analysis

Performance Graphs

Payroll History (in millions)

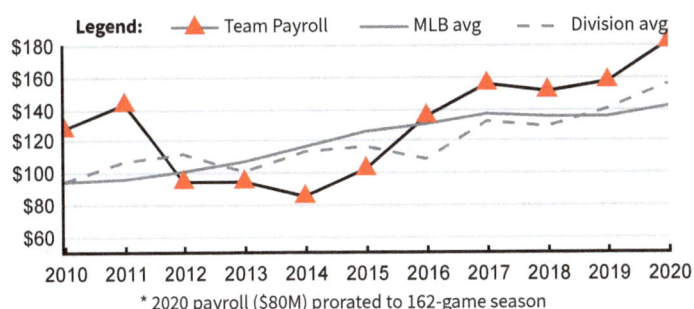

* 2020 payroll ($80M) prorated to 162-game season

Future Commitments (in millions)

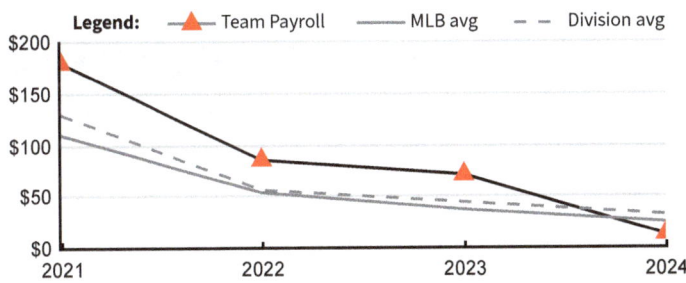

Farm System Ranking

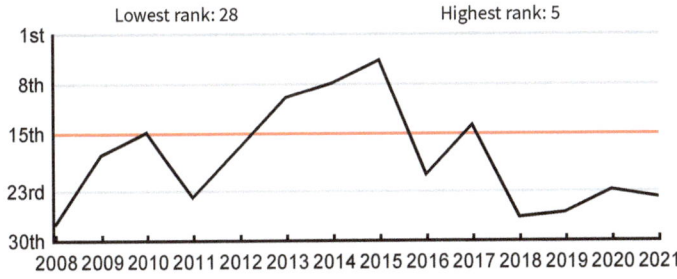

2020 Team Performance

ACTUAL STANDINGS

Team	W	L	Pct
ATL	35	25	0.583
MIA	31	29	0.517
PHI	28	32	0.467
NYM	**26**	**34**	**0.433**
WAS	26	34	0.433

dWIN% STANDINGS

Team	W	L	Pct
PHI	34	26	0.580
ATL	33	27	0.562
NYM	**32**	**28**	**0.549**
WAS	27	33	0.450
MIA	25	35	0.431

TOP HITTERS

Player	WARP
Jeff McNeil	1.1
Michael Conforto	0.9
Brandon Nimmo	0.9

TOP PITCHERS

Player	WARP
Jacob deGrom	2.2
Rick Porcello	1.1
Edwin Díaz	1.0

VITAL STATISTICS

Statistic Name	Value	Rank
Pythagenpat	.464	20th
dWin%	.549	6th
Runs Scored per Game	4.77	13th
Runs Allowed per Game	5.13	23rd
Deserved Runs Created Plus	105	6th
Deserved Run Average Minus	91	9th
Fielding Independent Pitching	4.47	15th
Defensive Efficiency Rating	.669	27th
Batter Age	28.2	16th
Pitcher Age	29.6	23rd
Payroll	$80.0M	3rd
Marginal $ per Marginal Win	$7.8M	28th

2021 Team Projections

PROJECTED STANDINGS

Team	W	L	Pct	+/-
NYM	93.6	68.4	0.578	23
Their additions should yield the best Mets team since 2015, even if their competition in the NL East is much stiffer than it was then.				
WAS	84.7	77.3	0.523	14
Mike Rizzo remade the middle of his lineup and improved the pitching staff, but given the caliber of their competition he could have aimed a hair higher.				
PHI	83.8	78.2	0.517	8
Re-signing J.T. Realmuto and Didi Gregorius keeps the offense intact, but has Dave Dombrowski successfully built a bullpen?				
ATL	81.5	80.5	0.503	-13
The rotation and positional stars set a high floor; their role players will determine their ceiling.				
MIA	70.9	91.1	0.438	-12
Hired a transformational leader and then did nothing to improve (or even reshape) a middling roster.				

TOP PROJECTED HITTERS

Player	WARP
Brandon Nimmo	4.1
Francisco Lindor	3.7
Michael Conforto	3.7

TOP PROJECTED PITCHERS

Player	WARP
Jacob deGrom	5.7
Carlos Carrasco	3.2
Noah Syndergaard	1.8

FARM SYSTEM REPORT

Top Prospect	Number of Top 101 Prospects
Ronny Mauricio, #42	3

KEY DEDUCTIONS

Player	WARP
Steven Matz	1.6
Michael Wacha	1.5
Amed Rosario	0.8
Andrés Giménez	0.7
Wilson Ramos	0.5

KEY ADDITIONS

New York Mets 2021

Player	WARP
Francisco Lindor	3.7
Carlos Carrasco	3.2
Marcus Stroman	1.8
James McCann	1.0
Joey Lucchesi	1.0
Jonathan Villar	0.8
Trevor May	0.8
Aaron Loup	0.5
Albert Almora Jr.	0.3
José Martínez	0.3

Team Personnel

President of BasebalL Operations
Sandy Alderson

General Manager
Jared Porter

Vice President, Assistant General Manager
Zack Scott

Vice President, International & Amateur Scouting
Tommy Tanous

Senior Director, Baseball Operations
Ian Levin

Manager
Luis Rojas

BP Alumni
Josh Turner

Citi Field Stats

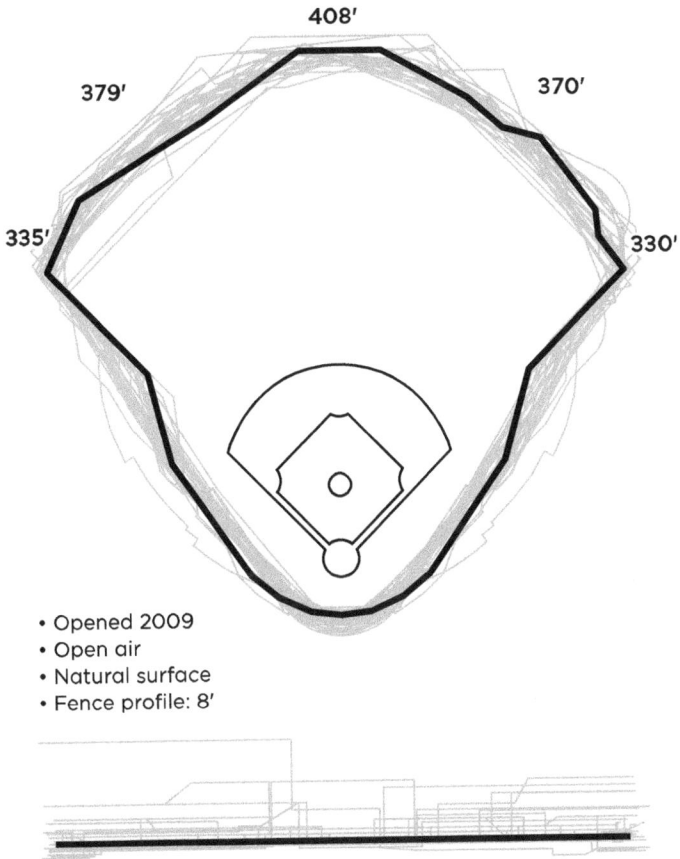

- Opened 2009
- Open air
- Natural surface
- Fence profile: 8'

Three-Year Park Factors

Runs	Runs/RH	Runs/LH	HR/RH	HR/LH
94	93	95	98	95

Mets Team Analysis

The nicest thing you can say about the Wilpons is that they always tried to win. The second nicest thing you can say is that they weren't very good at it.

Fred and Jeff Wilpon controlled the New York Mets for 17 seasons. They expected to make the playoffs each year, every summer serving as a perpetual push toward October no matter the circumstances. It was a relentlessly optimistic, borderline delusional mindset, one that demanded every player stay healthy and perform at peak level.

The Wilpon-led Mets made the postseason three times.

⚾ ⚾ ⚾

In 2006, hedge fund billionaire Steve Cohen agreed to purchase Picasso's "Le Rêve" for $139 million from casino tycoon Steve Wynn. Before the transaction was completed, Wynn inadvertently put his elbow through the painting's canvas while showing it off to a group of friends (including Nora Ephron and Barbara Walters). He decided that the mishap was a sign that he was supposed to keep the painting, and he had it restored instead of selling it.

Seven years later, Wynn decided to ignore the sign and move on from his damaged Picasso after all. Once again, Cohen was the buyer. He paid $155 million, considerably more than he was going to cough up for the piece in its original mint condition.

The Mets may not be a Picasso, but the Wilpons did enough damage to the franchise to give Cohen a healthy sense of déjà vu.

⚾ ⚾ ⚾

There's a famous scene from the 1980s that was immortalized in John Helyar's *Lords of the Realm*. Legend has it that then-commissioner Peter Ueberroth admonished the assembled group of MLB owners for wanting to hit a metaphorical red button that would win them the World Series at a deficit instead of hitting a black button that would make them a profit. In the ensuing decades, more and more owners have prioritized the black button, profits over pennants.

In 1986, just weeks after the Mets won their most recent World Series, Fred Wilpon and his brother-in-law Saul Katz raised their stake in the franchise from a small minority share to half the team. For the next 15 years, the Brooklyn-born real estate investors tenuously existed as equal co-owners alongside publishing heir Nelson Doubleday. Wilpon ran the day-to-day operations of the team as CEO, while Doubleday influenced some larger moves, like the Mike Piazza trade.

By 2001, Doubleday wanted out. He decided to sell his half to the Wilpons in a deal that went through only after a messy public split, a lawsuit and intervention from then-MLB commissioner Bud Selig. Shortly after vacating his ownership perch, Doubleday told *The Star-Ledger* that Jeff Wilpon, since installed as Mets COO by his father, "has decided that he's going to learn how to run a baseball team and take over at the end of the year. Run for the hills, boys."

For a few years after taking full control, the Wilpons were red button owners. They ran a top-five payroll from 2003 to 2009, signing high-end free agents like Carlos Beltrán and Pedro Martinez, and trading for expensive stars like Johan Santana and Carlos Delgado. Sure, there were warning signs—Martinez recounted in his autobiography how Jeff Wilpon pressured him to pitch with an injured toe to protect a big gate—and gossip about the Wilpons' meddling and micromanagement became frequent tabloid and talk radio fodder. But baseball fans can generally be mollified if you spend some money and contend for the playoffs, and the Wilpons did the bare minimum.

Then, close friend of the family Bernie Madoff got busted for running the largest Ponzi scheme in history. The Wilpons had around $500 million caught up in the con, and by the time the 2000s were over it was clear that their ability to play big-market baseball owners had been propped up by fictitious profits from the scam. When that house of cards crumbled, so too did the baseball team living in the penthouse.

General manager Sandy Alderson got to deal with the Madoff mess on the other side. Hired in 2010 at the urging of Selig to stabilize the front office, the longtime baseball consigliere tried to build a winner under the worst of circumstances. Despite constant proclamations from ownership that baseball operations wouldn't be affected by the Madoff scandal, payroll plummeted, from second in the majors at the start of the 2009 season to 25th six years later. Every now and again, you would hear that the team was just about to turn the corner, to go back to being a big spender. It never happened. Worse, it wasn't always clear how much the team had to spend at any given time, as debt service and financial restructuring took priority over the on-field product, leading to a scattershot decision-making process. The Wilpons still wanted to win and forced short-sighted moves towards contention, but they couldn't or wouldn't hit the red button anymore.

As the analytics boom of the 2010s progressed, the Mets were left on the sidelines. They forewent major technology spending, passing on investments like motion capture, TrackMan and high-speed cameras as other teams bet on their futures. They ran one of the smallest research-and-development shops in the game, employing only a handful of analysts at any given time as other front offices staffed up by the dozen. They fell years behind the analytics curve, even as they employed some of the brightest minds in the game. Their player development and acquisitions suffered for it.

Even though he was still heavily involved in the team, Fred Wilpon all but disappeared from the public eye after a disastrous 2011 profile in *The New Yorker*, rarely answering questions from the media. That left his son as the face of ownership, a scowling presence hovering over everything from big baseball moves like the Yoenis Céspedes trade—which Alderson sought his approval on before consummating minutes before the 2015 deadline—to minutiae like the wording of press releases about injuries. In a 2014 lawsuit, former Mets senior vice president Leigh Castergine alleged that, before she was fired, Jeff Wilpon told a meeting of Castergine and six male team executives that he was "as morally opposed to putting an e-cigarette sign in my ballpark as I am to Leigh having this baby without being married." The case was settled out of court before trial.

In the midst of the chaos, Alderson built a pennant winner in 2015 around homegrown pitching. But as the fates foretold, the LOLMets returned with new twists on classic hits; you may remember such tunes as "James Loney starting against Madison Bumgarner in the 2016 Wild Card Game" (that one ended in a shutout) and "we liked Eric Campbell's exit velocity, but it took us almost 200 games to notice he was smashing the ball into the ground, directly at fielders" (that one ended in a DFA after the 2016 season). Alderson's influence waned when the team went 70-92 in 2017; he took a medical leave of absence in June 2018, and the hiatus soon became permanent.

To replace one of the most accomplished front-office luminaries of his generation, the Mets hired agent Brodie Van Wagenen of CAA. He had no front office experience. As best as anyone could tell, his prime qualification for GM was that Jeff Wilpon liked talking baseball with him. Van Wagenen quickly proclaimed a fourth-place team as the divisional favorites, pawning off 2018 first-rounder Jarred Kelenic—now the No. 6 prospect in baseball—to bring in aging former client Robinson Canó and closer Edwin Díaz for a quick fix. After signing Jed Lowrie—another ex-client who would go on to total eight plate appearances during a two-year contract—Van Wagenen brashly told the rest of the NL East to "come get us."

They did.

New York Mets 2021

The high-water mark for the 2020 Mets was the night of August 28. As Game 2 of a seven-inning doubleheader at Yankee Stadium was underway, word leaked that Steve Cohen had, for the second time in less than a year, agreed to buy the team.

The prior December, Cohen had preliminarily agreed to purchase 80 percent of the Mets at a valuation of $2.6 million, with Fred Wilpon remaining the team's control person and Jeff staying on as COO for five more years. By February, the deal had fallen apart, or so it seemed. The *New York Post* reported that the Wilpons sought to retain more control over the team than Cohen was comfortable with, not just during the transition period but even beyond. The Wilpons re-opened the bidding, queuing up a months-long circus that included a bid from global pop icon Jennifer Lopez and fiancé/ESPN analyst/disgraced baseball legend Alex Rodriguez.

Cohen ended up with the team anyway, by virtue of being the richest person involved. Put simply, he wanted to buy his favorite baseball team, and he had the financial wherewithal to outbid all comers. But, instead of paying a little more the second time around, the way he did with the Picasso, this time Cohen paid a little less, just a hair under $2.5 billion—and, as a bonus, he immediately assumed full control of the team, without the five-year transitionary period from the original negotiations.

About an hour after the Cohen news broke, Amed Rosario walked off Aroldis Chapman to sweep the doubleheader. For several beats, nobody on the field realized it was a walkoff, since it was the seventh inning in the wrong ballpark. Such was baseball in 2020.

The win pulled the Mets into a playoff spot despite a middling 15-16 record. After further depleting a mediocre farm system for marginal upgrades around the edges, the team would sputter down the stretch one last time under Wilpon ownership. They would be eliminated on the last Saturday in September, in a season in which the playoff field was expanded and a .500 record would've earned entry as a wild card. At least the sun was finally, at last, rising over Citi Field again.

⚾   ⚾   ⚾

More than a month before officially assuming control of the team, Cohen announced that he was bringing Alderson back as team president, picking a decorated baseball executive to helm his franchise instead of a mediocre family member. Less than two hours after the sale closed in November, Alderson fired Van Wagenen.

Cohen and Alderson aimed high to replace the ousted ex-agent, initially seeking a big-name president of baseball operations. Cohen later admitted that they couldn't get permission from other teams to interview many of their top candidates. (Theo Epstein, the most sought-after unemployed executive in baseball, decided to take some time off.) So, they pivoted to finding a general manager to work under Alderson, eventually landing Arizona senior VP and assistant GM Jared Porter.

In Porter, they found a respected baseball lifer who embodies everything Van Wagenen was not. He has a long resume working in some of the best front offices in the game, winning four World Series rings under Epstein in both Boston and Chicago, the last two as pro scouting director. Where Van Wagenen's hiring was met with a collective LOLMets, Porter's was met with resounding praise from the baseball community.

⚾ ⚾ ⚾

The literal translation of "Le Rêve" is "the dream." Steve Cohen has an ambitious one: to win a World Series in the next three to five years.

Cohen has vowed to smash Ueberroth's red button in search of that dream—a welcome departure not only from the Wilpons, but the other owners who prefer the black button. The increased budget has already manifested across the organization, from small, subtle moves, like signing pitching prospect Sam McWilliams to the largest major-league contract ever given to a minor-league free agent with no service time, to early shopping in the free-agent gourmet aisle, as seen when they inked catcher James McCann to a four-year deal.

The Wilpons built Citi Field as a shrine to Branch Rickey's Brooklyn Dodgers, Fred's childhood favorite team. Cohen has instead pointed to the modern Dodgers—who have spent the better part of a decade building up a scouting, player development and analytics machine—as his artistic inspiration. The first step on that path is building a talented front office, and then stepping back and letting them do their jobs without the ownership interference that has long plagued the team. In the early going, Cohen has made all the right moves there; he's acted more like a passionate baseball fan, handing out bobbleheads and trading barbs on Twitter about bringing back Piazza-era black alternate jerseys and Old Timers' Day, than a micromanager who swears he knows better than the field staff and the front office.

It is said that Picasso painted "Le Rêve" in a day. The ball Mookie Wilson hit between Bill Buckner's legs—another piece in Cohen's collection and the closest thing to fine art the Mets have ever produced—was immortalized in an instant. Steve Cohen's dream to fly a World Series banner above Citi Field may take a little longer than either, but for now, anyway, it looks worth the wait. ⚾

—*Jarrett Seidler is an author of Baseball Prospectus.*

Part 2: Player Analysis

PLAYER COMMENTS WITH GRAPHS

Pete Alonso 1B
Born: 12/07/94 Age: 26 Bats: R Throws: R
Height: 6'3" Weight: 245 Origin: Round 2, 2016 Draft (#64 overall)

YEAR	TEAM	LVL	AGE	PA	R	2B	3B	HR	RBI	BB	K	SB	CS	AVG/OBP/SLG
2018	BNG	AA	23	273	42	12	0	15	52	43	50	0	2	.314/.440/.573
2018	LV	AAA	23	301	50	19	1	21	67	33	78	0	1	.260/.355/.585
2019	NYM	MLB	24	693	103	30	2	53	120	72	183	1	0	.260/.358/.583
2020	NYM	MLB	25	239	31	6	0	16	35	24	61	1	0	.231/.326/.490
2021 FS	NYM	MLB	26	600	98	25	1	40	105	61	161	0	1	.255/.351/.541
2021 DC	NYM	MLB	26	583	95	25	1	39	102	60	156	0	1	.255/.351/.541

Comparables: Fred McGriff, Ryan Howard, Matt Olson

At first glance, Alonso appears to have been the victim of the dreaded sophomore slump: A handful of his doubles transformed into singles, a few of his singles morphed into pop-ups, and his slash line looked more like that of Mike Napoli than Mark McGwire. But by the end of the shortened season, the Polar Bear looked like he was back in his element: outstanding power, a careful eye, and, *y'know, maybe we should mention that power again?* He even started making slightly more consistent contact on pitches in the zone, making it safe to assume that he'll be a dynamic middle-of-the-order slugger going forward.

YEAR	TEAM	LVL	AGE	PA	DRC+	BABIP	BRR	FRAA	WARP
2018	BNG	AA	23	273	177	.344	-1.6	1B(51): 1.8	2.2
2018	LV	AAA	23	301	121	.284	1.2	1B(59): 5.0	1.4
2019	NYM	MLB	24	693	140	.280	0.5	1B(156): 6.1	5.3
2020	NYM	MLB	25	239	106	.242	-2.3	1B(39): -4.3	0.1
2021 FS	NYM	MLB	26	600	137	.291	-0.9	1B 1	3.7
2021 DC	NYM	MLB	26	583	137	.291	-0.9	1B 1	3.6

Pete Alonso, continued

Batted Ball Distribution

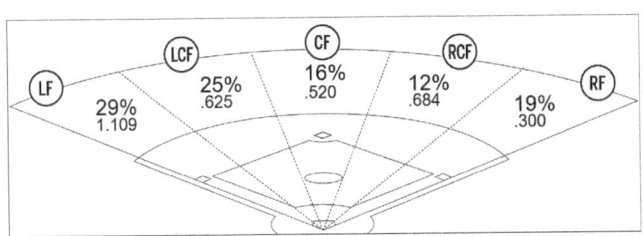

Strike Zone vs LHP   Strike Zone vs RHP

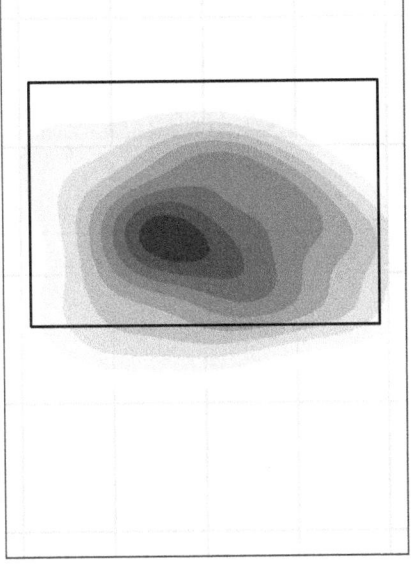

Robinson Canó 2B

Born: 10/22/82 Age: 38 Bats: L Throws: R
Height: 6'0" Weight: 212 Origin: International Free Agent, 2001

YEAR	TEAM	LVL	AGE	PA	R	2B	3B	HR	RBI	BB	K	SB	CS	AVG/OBP/SLG
2018	SEA	MLB	35	348	44	22	0	10	50	32	47	0	0	.303/.374/.471
2019	NYM	MLB	36	423	46	28	0	13	39	25	69	0	0	.256/.307/.428
2020	NYM	MLB	37	182	23	9	0	10	30	9	24	0	0	.316/.352/.544
2021 FS	NYM	MLB	38	600	66	27	0	21	74	39	105	0	1	.257/.315/.423

Comparables: Jeff Kent, Ian Kinsler, Chase Utley

This was supposed to be the place where you read about Canó's late-career resurgence in Queens. You know, a couple of quick sentences espousing how his bat looked more like Year Five than Year 15 of his no-doubt Hall of Fame career, and maybe a quick hit on his well-documented clubhouse presence. Instead, another PED suspension will cost the veteran second-sacker his 2021 season, $24 million dollars, and quite possibly his plaque in Cooperstown. While Sandy Alderson's new front office might enjoy being able to reinvest some of Canó's immediate salary, there's no silver lining for the player himself. Though he has done a remarkable job of keeping his skills sharp to this point, he'll likely be returning in 2022 for his age-39 season while trying to shake off the rust of a lost year and the bad feelings of a jilted New York fanbase.

YEAR	TEAM	LVL	AGE	PA	DRC+	BABIP	BRR	FRAA	WARP
2018	SEA	MLB	35	348	124	.329	-0.4	2B(69): -2.5, 1B(14): 0.3, 3B(2): 0.1	1.8
2019	NYM	MLB	36	423	89	.280	-0.7	2B(99): -7.4	0.0
2020	NYM	MLB	37	182	113	.319	-1.2	2B(34): -0.9	0.6
2021 FS	NYM	MLB	38	600	98	.286	-1.0	2B -2, 1B 0	1.3

Robinson Canó, continued

Batted Ball Distribution

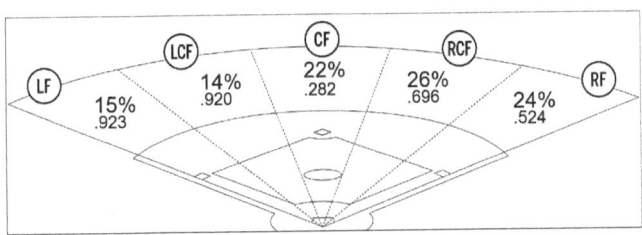

Strike Zone vs LHP

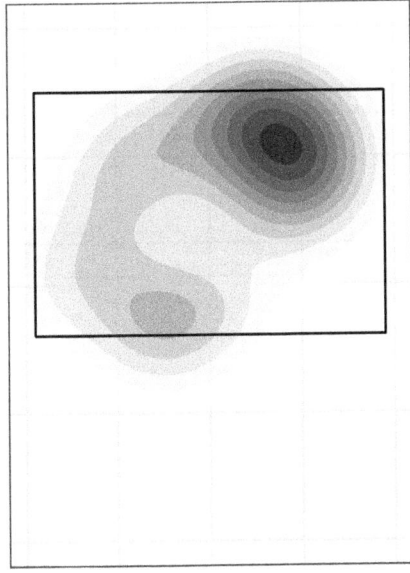

Strike Zone vs RHP

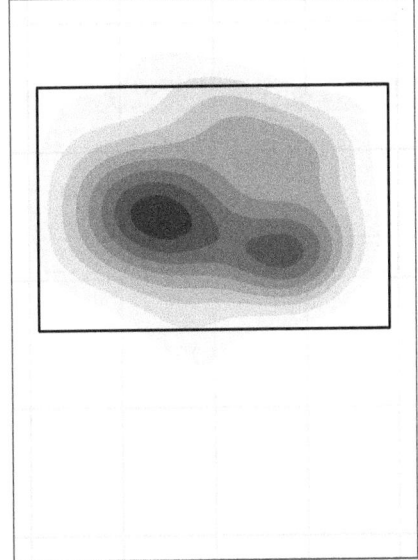

Robinson Chirinos C

Born: 06/05/84 Age: 37 Bats: R Throws: R
Height: 6'1" Weight: 220 Origin: International Free Agent, 2000

YEAR	TEAM	LVL	AGE	PA	R	2B	3B	HR	RBI	BB	K	SB	CS	AVG/OBP/SLG
2018	TEX	MLB	34	426	48	15	1	18	65	45	140	2	0	.222/.338/.419
2019	HOU	MLB	35	437	57	22	1	17	58	51	125	1	2	.238/.347/.443
2020	NYM	MLB	36	33	1	2	0	1	5	1	9	0	0	.219/.242/.375
2020	TEX	MLB	36	49	3	1	0	0	2	5	12	0	0	.119/.224/.143
2021 FS	*NYM*	*MLB*	*37*	*600*	*65*	*19*	*1*	*20*	*67*	*60*	*184*	*2*	*2*	*.201/.306/.359*

Comparables: Doug Mirabelli, David Ross, Jason Varitek

After half a decade as one of the game's most underrated offensive catchers, Chirinos' career took a sharp downward turn upon his return to his old Arlington stomping grounds. *Pelo Buche* may have value to some teams as a clubhouse presence and wearer-of-pads, but this looks like the end of the road.

YEAR	TEAM	P. COUNT	FRM RUNS	BLK RUNS	THRW RUNS	TOT RUNS
2018	TEX	15216	-11.2	0.7	-0.8	-11.3
2019	HOU	15758	-3.5	5.8	-0.5	1.9
2020	TEX	1958	-1.1	0.0	0.1	-1.1
2020	NYM	1580	-0.9	0.0	0.0	-0.9
2021	NYM	16650	-14.8	4.9	-0.4	-10.4
2021	NYM	16650	-14.8	1.7	-0.4	-13.5

YEAR	TEAM	LVL	AGE	PA	DRC+	BABIP	BRR	FRAA	WARP
2018	TEX	MLB	34	426	106	.304	-1.4	C(108): -10.8	1.2
2019	HOU	MLB	35	437	100	.306	-0.1	C(112): 3.0	2.6
2020	NYM	MLB	36	33	73	.273	0.0	C(12): -0.2	-0.1
2020	TEX	MLB	36	49	69	.161	-0.5	C(13): 0.3	-0.2
2021 FS	*NYM*	*MLB*	*37*	*600*	*84*	*.268*	*-0.7*	*C -10*	*0.2*

Robinson Chirinos, continued

Batted Ball Distribution

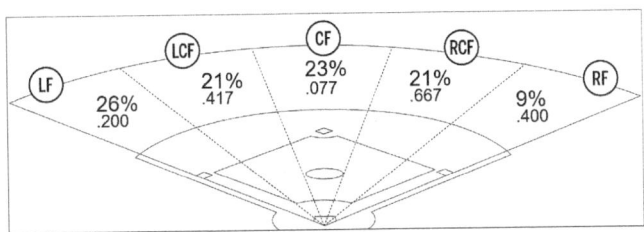

Strike Zone vs LHP   ### Strike Zone vs RHP

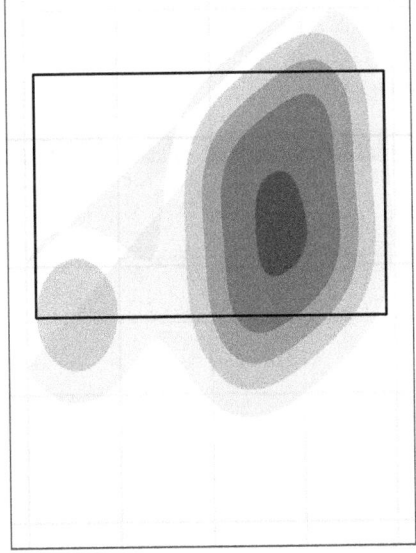

Michael Conforto RF

Born: 03/01/93   Age: 28   Bats: L   Throws: R
Height: 6'1"   Weight: 215   Origin: Round 1, 2014 Draft (#10 overall)

YEAR	TEAM	LVL	AGE	PA	R	2B	3B	HR	RBI	BB	K	SB	CS	AVG/OBP/SLG
2018	NYM	MLB	25	638	78	25	1	28	82	84	159	3	4	.243/.350/.448
2019	NYM	MLB	26	648	90	29	1	33	92	84	149	7	2	.257/.363/.494
2020	NYM	MLB	27	233	40	12	0	9	31	24	57	3	3	.322/.412/.515
2021 FS	NYM	MLB	28	600	94	26	1	27	89	72	153	4	2	.257/.362/.474
2021 DC	NYM	MLB	28	596	93	26	1	27	89	71	152	4	2	.257/.362/.474

Comparables: Pat Burrell, Dan Pasqua, Phil Plantier

A few years ago, it was opined that "every team has a Michael Conforto." *They should be so lucky.* In 2020, Conforto stayed healthy and was the lifeblood of the Mets' offense. Not only did he lead the team in games played and plate appearances while poking around near the top of several NL offensive leaderboards, he showed off his glove as an outstanding right fielder. (Seriously. Go check out his balletic catch on September 9 that ended up as one of the team's top defensive plays for the season.) No longer a quiet star, Conforto plays louder than his soft-spoken demeanor. With free agency impending at the end of the 2021 season and a prime platform year looming, all those teams that don't have a Michael Conforto may want to shell out big bucks to get one of their own.

YEAR	TEAM	LVL	AGE	PA	DRC+	BABIP	BRR	FRAA	WARP
2018	NYM	MLB	25	638	112	.289	-4.2	LF(84): 1.1, CF(58): -7.3, RF(13): 0.1	1.8
2019	NYM	MLB	26	648	122	.290	-0.3	RF(132): 10.0, CF(39): -3.7	4.1
2020	NYM	MLB	27	233	120	.412	-0.5	RF(52): -3.1	0.9
2021 FS	NYM	MLB	28	600	126	.317	-0.6	RF 5, CF -1	4.0
2021 DC	NYM	MLB	28	596	126	.317	-0.6	RF 5, CF -1	3.7

Michael Conforto, continued

Batted Ball Distribution

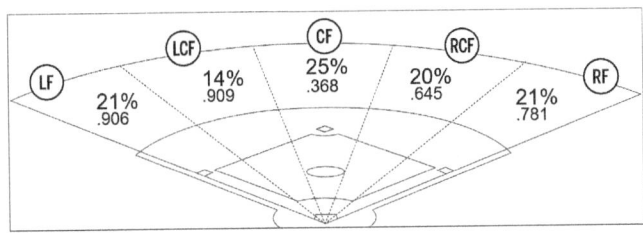

Strike Zone vs LHP   Strike Zone vs RHP

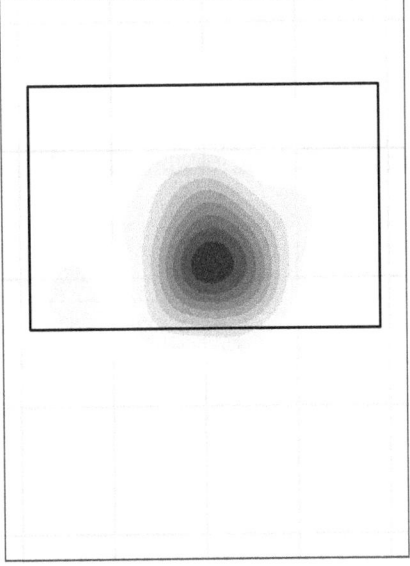

J.D. Davis LF

Born: 04/27/93 Age: 28 Bats: R Throws: R
Height: 6'3" Weight: 218 Origin: Round 3, 2014 Draft (#75 overall)

YEAR	TEAM	LVL	AGE	PA	R	2B	3B	HR	RBI	BB	K	SB	CS	AVG/OBP/SLG
2018	FRE	AAA	25	377	56	25	2	17	81	36	69	3	0	.342/.406/.583
2018	HOU	MLB	25	113	9	2	0	1	5	10	29	0	0	.175/.248/.223
2019	NYM	MLB	26	453	65	22	1	22	57	38	97	3	0	.307/.369/.527
2020	NYM	MLB	27	229	26	9	0	6	19	31	56	0	0	.247/.371/.389
2021 FS	NYM	MLB	28	600	83	26	1	25	86	58	161	1	1	.249/.332/.443
2021 DC	NYM	MLB	28	596	83	26	1	24	86	57	160	1	1	.249/.332/.443

Comparables: Fernando Tatis, Dean Palmer, Hank Blalock

When the Mets move a defensively-challenged hitter into left field to shoehorn them into the lineup, the outcomes typically range somewhere between unintentionally hilarious (Todd Hundley) or downright sad (Lucas Duda). While both Davis and Dominic Smith served some time in the Hundley-Duda Memorial Pit of Despair, Davis not only showed his limitations on the grass, but also saw his offensive production peter out as well. At his best, his right-handed batted ball profile and production make for a valuable lineup cog, but he'll be best served at a position where he can focus on what he does well offensively, not how much work he needs with a glove. Still, he's proven that he can be an adequate big-league regular, provided his time in left field is minimal.

YEAR	TEAM	LVL	AGE	PA	DRC+	BABIP	BRR	FRAA	WARP
2018	FRE	AAA	25	377	162	.385	0.0	3B(51): 4.2, LF(11): -0.8, RF(11): -0.3	3.6
2018	HOU	MLB	25	113	67	.233	-0.5	3B(23): 0.9, 1B(13): 0.0, LF(5): 0.6	0.0
2019	NYM	MLB	26	453	121	.355	0.4	LF(79): -4.9, 3B(31): -0.5	2.1
2020	NYM	MLB	27	229	103	.318	-0.5	3B(34): -0.2, LF(8): -0.4	0.4
2021 FS	NYM	MLB	28	600	108	.311	-0.9	3B 1, LF 0	1.9
2021 DC	NYM	MLB	28	596	108	.311	-0.9	3B 1, LF 0	1.8

J.D. Davis, continued

Batted Ball Distribution

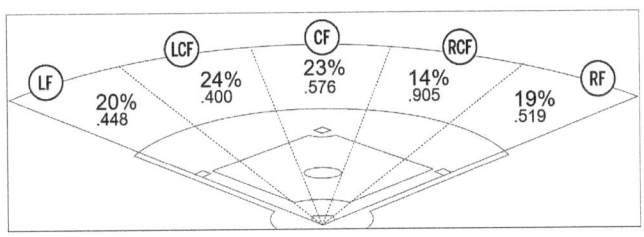

Strike Zone vs LHP   Strike Zone vs RHP

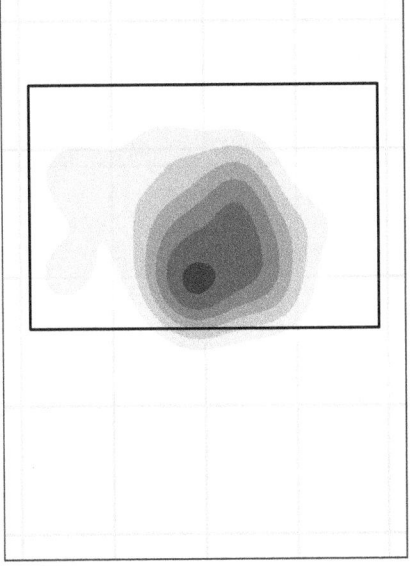

Todd Frazier 3B

Born: 02/12/86 Age: 35 Bats: R Throws: R
Height: 6'3" Weight: 220 Origin: Round 1, 2007 Draft (#34 overall)

YEAR	TEAM	LVL	AGE	PA	R	2B	3B	HR	RBI	BB	K	SB	CS	AVG/OBP/SLG
2018	NYM	MLB	32	472	54	18	0	18	59	48	112	9	4	.213/.303/.390
2019	STL	HI-A	33	43	3	0	0	1	8	6	8	0	1	.216/.326/.297
2019	NYM	MLB	33	499	63	19	2	21	67	40	106	1	2	.251/.329/.443
2020	NYM	MLB	34	51	5	2	0	2	5	1	16	0	0	.224/.255/.388
2020	TEX	MLB	34	121	11	7	1	2	7	10	26	1	1	.241/.322/.380
2021 FS	NYM	MLB	35	600	67	25	1	23	74	55	156	7	4	.219/.306/.402
2021 DC	NYM	MLB	35	264	29	11	0	10	32	24	68	3	2	.219/.306/.402

Comparables: Dean Palmer, Casey Blake, Eric Hinske

For someone nicknamed "The ToddFather," Frazier sure seems to have difficulty ordering hits these days.

YEAR	TEAM	LVL	AGE	PA	DRC+	BABIP	BRR	FRAA	WARP
2018	NYM	MLB	32	472	99	.241	2.5	3B(109): 5.9	2.5
2019	STL	HI-A	33	43	116	.250	0.1	3B(10): 1.1, 1B(5): -0.1, SS(3): -0.1	0.3
2019	NYM	MLB	33	499	103	.284	0.0	3B(120): 6.5, 1B(3): 0.1	2.7
2020	NYM	MLB	34	51	98	.290	0.3	3B(14): 1.2, P(1): -0.0	0.3
2020	TEX	MLB	34	121	93	.300	-0.2	1B(16): -0.6, 3B(15): -0.7	-0.1
2021 FS	NYM	MLB	35	600	93	.265	-0.1	1B 0, 3B 0	0.6
2021 DC	NYM	MLB	35	264	93	.265	0.0	1B 0, 3B 0	0.2

Todd Frazier, continued

Batted Ball Distribution

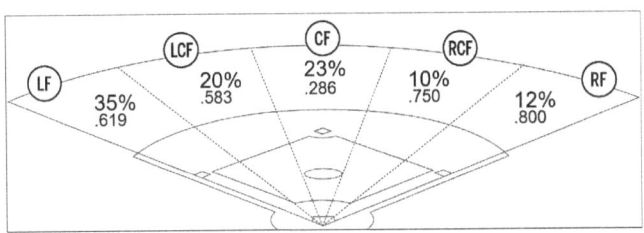

Strike Zone vs LHP

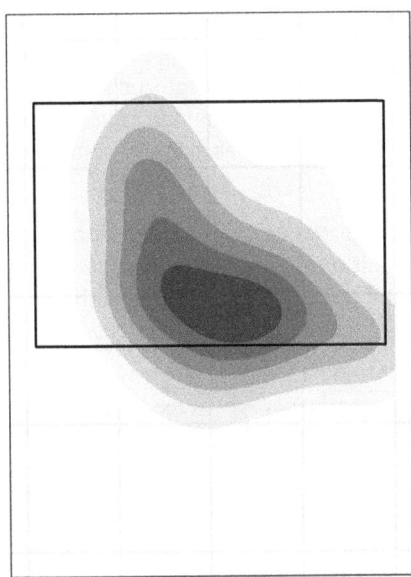

Strike Zone vs RHP

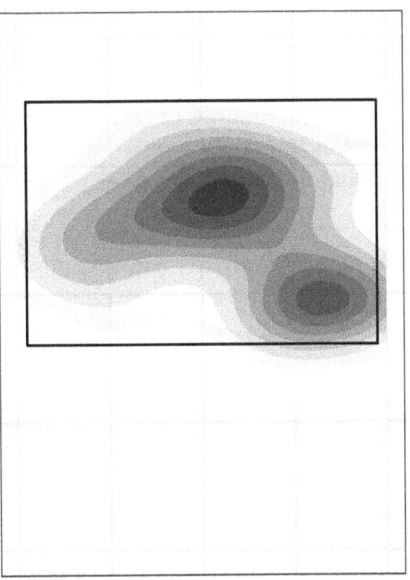

Type	Frequency	Velocity	H Movement	V Movement
● Fastball	61.5%	64.2 [10]	-7.8 [95]	-42.8 [22]
✳ Knuckleball	38.5%	54.7 [89]	2.2 [111]	-81.1 [89]

Francisco Lindor SS

Born: 11/14/93 Age: 27 Bats: S Throws: R
Height: 5'11" Weight: 190 Origin: Round 1, 2011 Draft (#8 overall)

YEAR	TEAM	LVL	AGE	PA	R	2B	3B	HR	RBI	BB	K	SB	CS	AVG/OBP/SLG
2018	CLE	MLB	24	745	129	42	2	38	92	70	107	25	10	.277/.352/.519
2019	CLE	MLB	25	654	101	40	2	32	74	46	98	22	5	.284/.335/.518
2020	CLE	MLB	26	266	30	13	0	8	27	24	41	6	2	.258/.335/.415
2021 FS	NYM	MLB	27	600	94	31	1	27	88	53	98	15	6	.269/.342/.485
2021 DC	NYM	MLB	27	619	96	32	1	28	91	55	101	15	6	.269/.342/.485

Comparables: Aledmys Díaz, Cal Ripken Jr., Troy Tulowitzki

Shortly after Cleveland's playoff exit, Lindor was asked whether they could afford to extend him. The response? "Of course. It's a billion-dollar team." There was a wry smile on his face, conscious of the cartoonish predictability of the team's financial decisions; he might as well be asking Scrooge McDuck for a deal. Lindor shares the youthful, exuberant spirit of Huey, Dewey and Louie, but he hasn't melted the hearts of ownership. On *DuckTales*, this particular adventure would end with Lindor landing the treasure he so richly deserves and reuniting with his baseball family. If you head down to Progressive Field over the offseason, you might instead catch the bespectacled Dolan clan, complete with top hats and spats, performing a surprisingly passable synchronized backstroke through the mounds of cash saved by not extending their franchise shortstop. Cleveland fans might wish that were so anyway; humor has a way of softening the edges of disappointment.

The owner of Lindor's new squad has a bigger vat of cash to swim through and doesn't seem to mind spending some of it on a competitive baseball team. Cleveland fans are going to need to hire personal comedians to follow them around if they want humor to dull the pain of watching Lindor flash his trademark smile all year in New York.

YEAR	TEAM	LVL	AGE	PA	DRC+	BABIP	BRR	FRAA	WARP
2018	CLE	MLB	24	745	127	.279	-0.5	SS(157): 5.9	6.5
2019	CLE	MLB	25	654	117	.291	-2.3	SS(137): -4.8	3.8
2020	CLE	MLB	26	266	120	.280	-0.4	SS(58): -0.2	1.4
2021 FS	NYM	MLB	27	600	121	.286	0.7	SS 0	3.6
2021 DC	NYM	MLB	27	619	121	.286	0.7	SS 0	3.7

Francisco Lindor, continued

Batted Ball Distribution

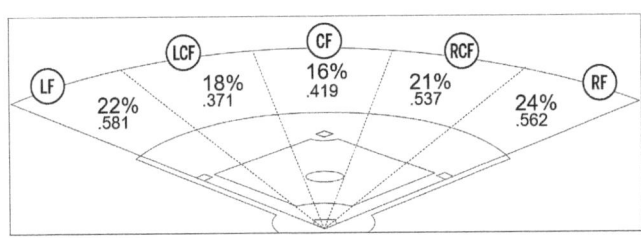

Strike Zone vs LHP   Strike Zone vs RHP

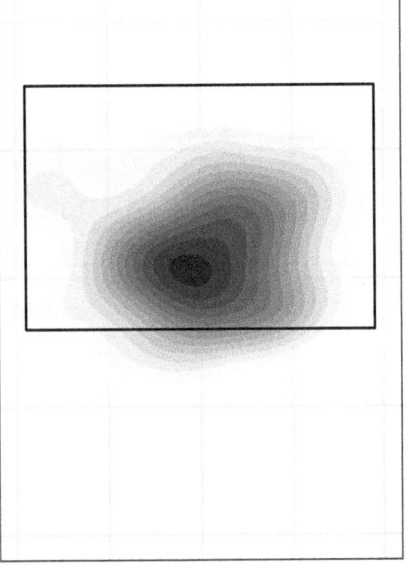

Jake Marisnick CF

Born: 03/30/91   Age: 30   Bats: R   Throws: R
Height: 6'4"   Weight: 220   Origin: Round 3, 2009 Draft (#104 overall)

YEAR	TEAM	LVL	AGE	PA	R	2B	3B	HR	RBI	BB	K	SB	CS	AVG/OBP/SLG
2018	FRE	AAA	27	82	18	8	2	4	13	6	17	3	1	.342/.402/.671
2018	HOU	MLB	27	235	34	8	1	10	28	15	84	6	2	.211/.275/.399
2019	HOU	MLB	28	318	46	16	3	10	34	17	95	10	3	.233/.289/.411
2020	NYM	MLB	29	34	4	3	0	2	5	1	10	0	0	.333/.353/.606
2021 FS	NYM	MLB	30	600	63	23	2	23	73	38	196	16	7	.216/.280/.392
2021 DC	NYM	MLB	30	157	16	6	0	6	19	10	51	4	2	.216/.280/.392

Comparables: Brandon Barnes, Michael A. Taylor, Laynce Nix

Acquired in the offseason to be something of a platoon partner for Brandon Nimmo, Marisnick's combination of outstanding defense and occasional ability to punish a left-handed pitcher should have balanced out the lineup while providing sorely needed outs for the pitching staff. Instead, the team saw precious little of their new addition's glove (and flow) as hamstring injuries limited him to just 16 games. He put up outstanding numbers in his limited game action last season thanks to a power surge, but the underlying strikeout issues probably make him most desirable in a role similar to the one he had on the Astros: the fourth or fifth outfielder on a good team.

YEAR	TEAM	LVL	AGE	PA	DRC+	BABIP	BRR	FRAA	WARP
2018	FRE	AAA	27	82	168	.396	-0.5	CF(12): -2.3, RF(6): 0.9	0.5
2018	HOU	MLB	27	235	79	.292	2.3	CF(96): -5.7, LF(1): -0.0, RF(1): -0.0	-0.1
2019	HOU	MLB	28	318	67	.310	0.8	CF(109): 7.7	0.7
2020	NYM	MLB	29	34	87	.429	-0.1	CF(16): 1.5	0.1
2021 FS	NYM	MLB	30	600	81	.290	1.4	CF 2, RF 1	0.8
2021 DC	NYM	MLB	30	157	81	.290	0.4	CF 1, RF 0	0.2

Jake Marisnick, continued

Batted Ball Distribution

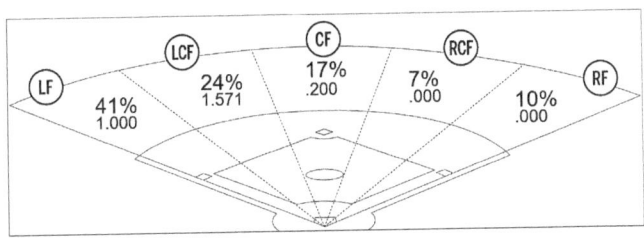

Strike Zone vs LHP   Strike Zone vs RHP

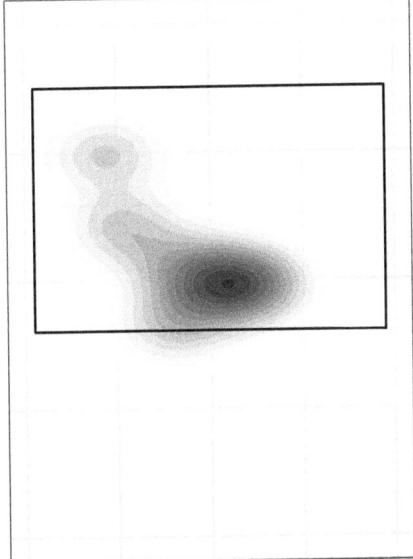

José Martínez OF

Born: 07/25/88 Age: 32 Bats: R Throws: R
Height: 6'6" Weight: 215 Origin: International Free Agent, 2006

YEAR	TEAM	LVL	AGE	PA	R	2B	3B	HR	RBI	BB	K	SB	CS	AVG/OBP/SLG
2018	STL	MLB	29	590	64	30	0	17	83	49	104	0	3	.305/.364/.457
2019	STL	MLB	30	373	45	13	2	10	42	35	82	3	0	.269/.340/.410
2020	TB	MLB	31	76	10	4	0	2	10	9	20	0	0	.239/.329/.388
2020	CHC	MLB	31	22	0	0	0	0	0	1	7	0	0	.000/.045/.000
2021 FS	NYM	MLB	32	600	76	26	1	19	78	57	143	2	2	.246/.323/.406
2021 DC	NYM	MLB	32	240	30	10	0	7	31	23	57	0	1	.246/.323/.406

Comparables: Shawn Green, Andre Ethier, Bubba Trammell

The other guy the Rays acquired in the Randy Arozarena trade had a slightly less memorable season. In a month with Tampa, Martínez failed to do what he was acquired to do: hit lefties. He was shipped at the deadline to the Cubs for an actual prospect and he was soon thereafter jettisoned to the alternate site after 22 hitless plate appearances, never to be seen by the Wrigley faithful—er, bleachers—again. Martínez's track record against lefties should net him another big-league job by the time you read this.

YEAR	TEAM	LVL	AGE	PA	DRC+	BABIP	BRR	FRAA	WARP
2018	STL	MLB	29	590	118	.351	-3.6	1B(84): -10.4, RF(46): 0.2	0.9
2019	STL	MLB	30	373	94	.328	0.7	RF(75): -3.5, LF(7): -0.0	0.3
2020	TB	MLB	31	76	76	.311	0.0	1B(6): 0.0	-0.1
2020	CHC	MLB	31	22	73	.000			0.0
2021 FS	NYM	MLB	32	600	99	.302	-0.7	RF 0, 1B 0	0.8
2021 DC	NYM	MLB	32	240	99	.302	-0.3	RF 0	0.3

José Martínez, continued

Batted Ball Distribution

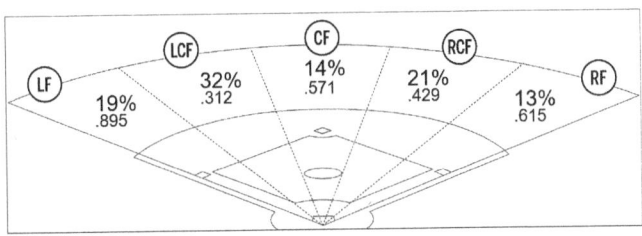

Strike Zone vs LHP   Strike Zone vs RHP

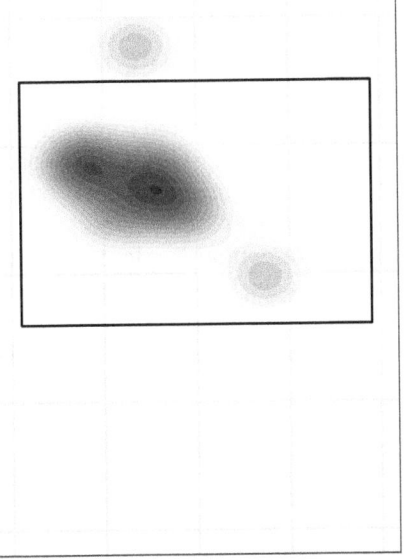

James McCann C

Born: 06/13/90 Age: 31 Bats: R Throws: R
Height: 6'3" Weight: 220 Origin: Round 2, 2011 Draft (#76 overall)

YEAR	TEAM	LVL	AGE	PA	R	2B	3B	HR	RBI	BB	K	SB	CS	AVG/OBP/SLG
2018	DET	MLB	28	457	31	16	0	8	39	26	116	0	3	.220/.267/.314
2019	CHW	MLB	29	476	62	26	1	18	60	30	137	4	1	.273/.328/.460
2020	CHW	MLB	30	111	20	3	0	7	15	8	30	1	1	.289/.360/.536
2021 FS	NYM	MLB	31	600	75	26	1	22	82	39	169	2	2	.246/.307/.423
2021 DC	NYM	MLB	31	429	53	19	0	16	58	28	120	2	1	.246/.307/.423

Comparables: Randy Knorr, Nick Hundley, Damian Miller

YEAR	TEAM	P. COUNT	FRM RUNS	BLK RUNS	THRW RUNS	TOT RUNS
2018	DET	16729	-2.3	-1.4	1.1	-2.6
2019	CHW	15359	-8.0	-0.9	0.9	-8.0
2020	CHW	4053	1.5	0.0	0.0	1.5
2021	NYM	14430	-3.2	-0.6	0.2	-3.5
2021	NYM	14430	-3.2	-0.3	0.2	-3.3

In a masterstroke of innovation, the Tigers non-tendered McCann, their former second-round pick, at the end of the 2018 season. The massive insult of being cast off by a horrid rebuilding team spurred McCann to the best offensive season of his career in 2019, and his first All-Star Game appearance. Tapping into the power of injustice, the White Sox insulted McCann again, signing Yasmani Grandal in November of 2019 and handing him McCann's starting job. In a heavily-used backup role, McCann improved even more offensively, and arrested career-long struggles at pitch-framing to boot. After inking him to a four-year, $40 million deal, the Mets will receive an increasingly solid all-around backstop, but will be wasting their money if they do not seek out a new, galling way to draw his ire and fuel his hunger for a revenge tour. If a club unceremoniously releases him in spring training, it may well produce an MVP campaign, just, you know, for another team.

YEAR	TEAM	LVL	AGE	PA	DRC+	BABIP	BRR	FRAA	WARP
2018	DET	MLB	28	457	72	.282	-4.2	C(114): -5.0	-0.3
2019	CHW	MLB	29	476	95	.359	-0.1	C(106): -10.2	1.0
2020	CHW	MLB	30	111	112	.339	-0.5	C(30): 0.1	0.7
2021 FS	NYM	MLB	31	600	97	.314	-0.7	C -5	1.7
2021 DC	NYM	MLB	31	429	97	.314	-0.5	C -4	1.0

James McCann, continued

Batted Ball Distribution

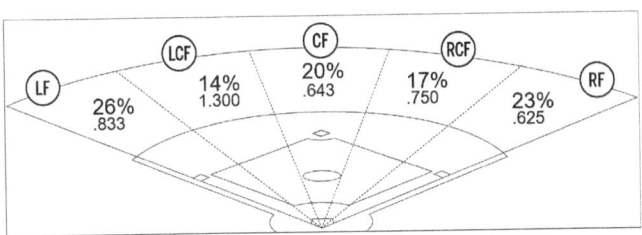

Strike Zone vs LHP   Strike Zone vs RHP

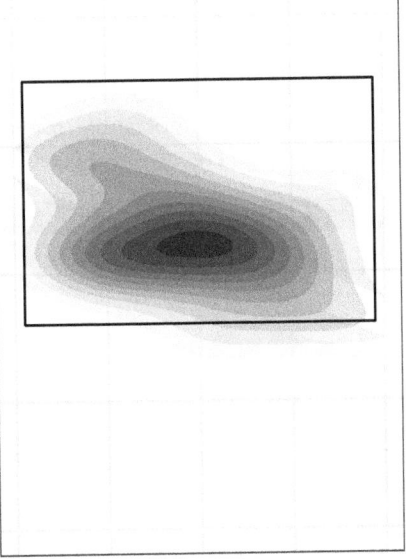

Jeff McNeil 3B

Born: 04/08/92   Age: 29   Bats: L   Throws: R
Height: 6'1"   Weight: 195   Origin: Round 12, 2013 Draft (#356 overall)

YEAR	TEAM	LVL	AGE	PA	R	2B	3B	HR	RBI	BB	K	SB	CS	AVG/OBP/SLG
2018	BNG	AA	26	241	49	16	3	14	43	22	23	3	0	.327/.402/.626
2018	LV	AAA	26	143	23	10	2	5	28	14	19	3	0	.368/.427/.600
2018	NYM	MLB	26	248	35	11	6	3	19	14	24	7	1	.329/.381/.471
2019	NYM	MLB	27	567	83	38	1	23	75	35	75	5	6	.318/.384/.531
2020	NYM	MLB	28	209	19	14	0	4	23	20	24	0	2	.311/.383/.454
2021 FS	NYM	MLB	29	600	90	30	2	20	85	45	86	6	3	.285/.358/.463
2021 DC	NYM	MLB	29	604	91	30	2	20	86	45	87	6	3	.285/.358/.463

Comparables: Ian Kinsler, Chase Utley, Jose Altuve

While filling in across the diamond and jump-starting the team's offense, the Mets' resident Swiss Army knife also does the little things well. McNeil endeared himself to fans by adopting puppies and giving Joe West the business, and won over his teammates by talking up his manager and putting his body on the line to make ill-conceived, Kool-Aid Man-adjacent catches in the outfield. But for all the little things, McNeil's bread and butter is still one very, very big thing: He reaches base almost 40 percent of the time, making hard contact while hardly ever striking out. After three years of continued production (and a hot September waylaying a cold August's concerns), Six has established himself as perhaps the most important factor among the team's position players, the one thing they should never leave Queens without.

YEAR	TEAM	LVL	AGE	PA	DRC+	BABIP	BRR	FRAA	WARP
2018	BNG	AA	26	241	174	.316	1.7	2B(47): 3.9, 3B(9): -0.6, SS(3): -0.3	2.9
2018	LV	AAA	26	143	156	.394	0.4	2B(24): -3.3, 3B(3): -0.1, LF(2): 0.1	0.9
2018	NYM	MLB	26	248	118	.359	0.8	2B(54): -2.6, 3B(4): 0.3	1.2
2019	NYM	MLB	27	567	128	.337	-2.7	LF(71): -5.2, RF(42): -1.2, 2B(37): -2.8	2.5
2020	NYM	MLB	28	209	117	.335	-1.4	LF(28): -1.5, 2B(12): 0.7, 3B(9): 2.5	1.1
2021 FS	NYM	MLB	29	600	123	.311	-0.1	2B -1, LF -2	3.1
2021 DC	NYM	MLB	29	604	123	.311	-0.1	2B -1, LF -2	3.1

Jeff McNeil, continued

Batted Ball Distribution

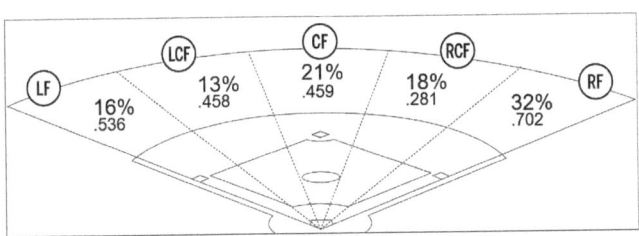

Strike Zone vs LHP   Strike Zone vs RHP

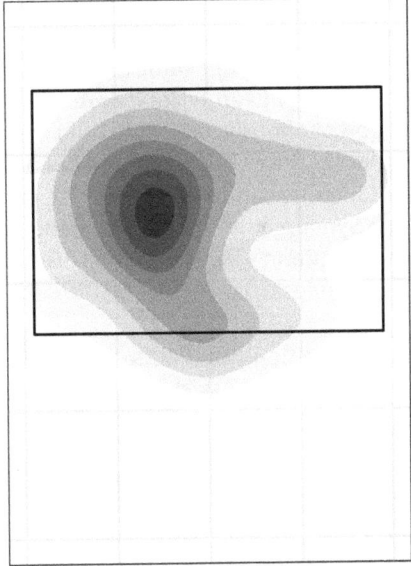

Tomás Nido C

Born: 04/12/94 Age: 27 Bats: R Throws: R
Height: 6'0" Weight: 211 Origin: Round 8, 2012 Draft (#260 overall)

YEAR	TEAM	LVL	AGE	PA	R	2B	3B	HR	RBI	BB	K	SB	CS	AVG/OBP/SLG
2018	BNG	AA	24	228	23	18	1	5	30	7	36	0	0	.274/.298/.437
2018	NYM	MLB	24	90	10	3	0	1	9	4	27	0	0	.167/.200/.238
2019	SYR	AAA	25	40	3	1	0	0	4	1	13	0	0	.289/.300/.316
2019	NYM	MLB	25	144	9	5	0	4	14	7	37	0	0	.191/.231/.316
2020	NYM	MLB	26	26	4	1	0	2	6	2	6	0	0	.292/.346/.583
2021 FS	NYM	MLB	27	600	69	23	1	17	71	33	157	0	1	.216/.263/.358
2021 DC	NYM	MLB	27	188	21	7	0	5	22	10	49	0	0	.216/.263/.358

Comparables: Chris Krug, Jim Campbell, John Orton

After starting the season firmly ensconced as the Mets' reserve catcher, Tomas Nido promptly did something nearly no one thought he would do: he hit. Of course it was a small sample size, even by backup catcher standards, but it included a charmed two-homer game and a solid line drive off of Aaron Nola. Even a little bit of offensive efficacy could make the talented receiver a major-league regular for the next decade, but unfortunately his chance for a breakout was cut short after he contracted COVID-19, ending his season. Given his previous role as Noah Syndergaard's personal catcher, the Mets are likely to keep him around as James McCann's backup in the hopes that his surge with the bat in 2020 was a sign of things to come.

YEAR	TEAM	P. COUNT	FRM RUNS	BLK RUNS	THRW RUNS	TOT RUNS
2018	NYM	3483	3.5	-0.1	0.0	3.4
2018	BNG	6635	7.7	0.0	0.5	8.0
2019	NYM	5589	5.3	0.4	-0.6	5.1
2019	SYR	1379	1.2	0.1	0.1	1.4
2020	NYM	1049	0.8	0.1	0.0	0.9
2021	NYM	6012	5.7	1.0	0.0	6.6
2021	NYM	6012	5.7	0.4	0.0	6.1

YEAR	TEAM	LVL	AGE	PA	DRC+	BABIP	BRR	FRAA	WARP
2018	BNG	AA	24	228	110	.303	-2.0	C(48): 8.5	1.6
2018	NYM	MLB	24	90	58	.224	0.2	C(30): 3.4	0.3
2019	SYR	AAA	25	40	79	.423	-1.2	C(11): 1.4	0.1
2019	NYM	MLB	25	144	58	.232	-1.5	C(48): 5.1	0.3
2020	NYM	MLB	26	26	102	.312	0.0	C(7): -0.1	0.1
2021 FS	NYM	MLB	27	600	66	.267	-0.9	C 16	1.4
2021 DC	NYM	MLB	27	188	66	.267	-0.3	C 7	0.6

Tomás Nido, continued

Batted Ball Distribution

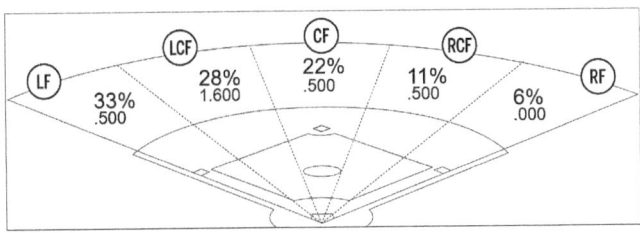

Strike Zone vs LHP   Strike Zone vs RHP

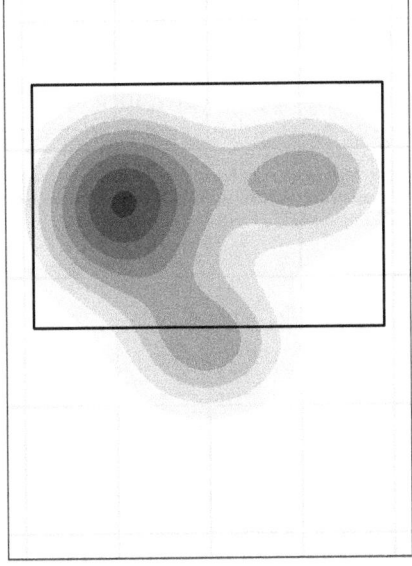

Brandon Nimmo CF
Born: 03/27/93   Age: 28   Bats: L   Throws: R
Height: 6'3"   Weight: 206   Origin: Round 1, 2011 Draft (#13 overall)

YEAR	TEAM	LVL	AGE	PA	R	2B	3B	HR	RBI	BB	K	SB	CS	AVG/OBP/SLG
2018	NYM	MLB	25	535	77	28	8	17	47	80	140	9	6	.263/.404/.483
2019	SYR	AAA	26	44	10	2	0	1	6	8	8	3	0	.200/.364/.343
2019	NYM	MLB	26	254	34	11	1	8	29	46	71	3	0	.221/.375/.407
2020	NYM	MLB	27	225	33	8	3	8	18	33	43	1	2	.280/.404/.484
2021 FS	NYM	MLB	28	600	98	27	4	19	66	85	143	5	2	.258/.383/.443
2021 DC	NYM	MLB	28	623	102	28	4	19	68	89	148	5	2	.258/.383/.443

Comparables: B.J. Upton, Jose Cruz, Don Lock

Trout, Soto, Votto, Freeman ... Nimmo. Since his debut in 2016, the Mets' center fielder has the fifth-highest on-base percentage among consistent MLB regulars, and the names most adjacent to him on this list are a veritable who's who of MVPs and All-Stars. The only thing he lacks compared to all the other names on the top 10 OBP list–which continues with the names Judge, Goldschmidt, Yelich, Harper, and Rendon–is power production; in that regard Nimmo remains miles away from his peers. Nevertheless, the man with the million-dollar smile remains an underrated offensive catalyst despite his limitations when it comes to speed, defense, and power. When he's able to put the ball in play regularly, such as during his healthy the 2018 and 2020 seasons, he's an outstanding regular, no matter where he's slotted in an outfield.

YEAR	TEAM	LVL	AGE	PA	DRC+	BABIP	BRR	FRAA	WARP
2018	NYM	MLB	25	535	122	.351	5.1	RF(62): 0.1, CF(44): -0.9, LF(32): 2.1	3.6
2019	SYR	AAA	26	44	100	.231	0.2	CF(8): 0.4, LF(2): -0.2	0.2
2019	NYM	MLB	26	254	100	.293	1.0	CF(43): -0.0, LF(38): -0.8, RF(6): 0.5	0.9
2020	NYM	MLB	27	225	123	.326	-1.5	CF(44): 0.0, LF(22): -2.2, RF(10): 0.1	0.9
2021 FS	NYM	MLB	28	600	127	.329	-0.1	LF 1, CF 1	3.9
2021 DC	NYM	MLB	28	623	127	.329	-0.1	LF 1, CF 1	4.1

Brandon Nimmo, continued

Batted Ball Distribution

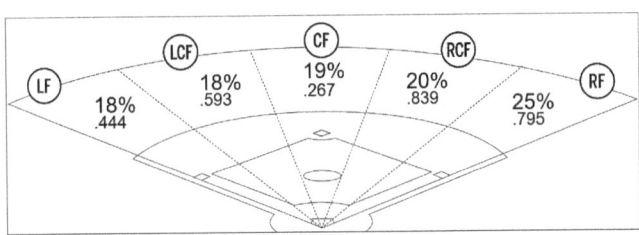

Strike Zone vs LHP   Strike Zone vs RHP

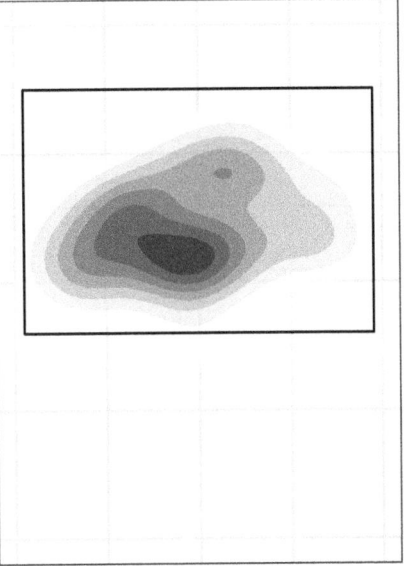

José Peraza SS

Born: 04/30/94 Age: 27 Bats: R Throws: R
Height: 6'0" Weight: 210 Origin: International Free Agent, 2010

YEAR	TEAM	LVL	AGE	PA	R	2B	3B	HR	RBI	BB	K	SB	CS	AVG/OBP/SLG
2018	CIN	MLB	24	683	85	31	4	14	58	29	75	23	6	.288/.326/.416
2019	CIN	MLB	25	403	37	18	2	6	33	17	58	7	6	.239/.285/.346
2020	BOS	MLB	26	120	13	8	1	1	8	5	18	1	1	.225/.275/.342
2021 FS	NYM	MLB	27	600	71	29	2	11	67	28	90	19	8	.264/.309/.389
2021 DC	NYM	MLB	27	64	7	3	0	1	7	2	9	1	1	.264/.309/.389

Comparables: Bill Spiers, Jean Segura, Yuniesky Betancourt

There's nothing worse than grabbing the wrong tool for the job. Ever try to use a Phillips head to fasten a straight screw? Build Ikea furniture with the wrong size Allen wrench? Use your plus-plus speed without knowing how to get on base? It's a terrible feeling. Though he was offered a clear path to consistent playing time, Peraza proved ill-equipped to get the job done. He did not hit well or field well, and he's never been known to pack a power tool. Peraza is mighty fast, it's true, but if you're only bringing one tool to the party, you better be able to put it to good use. Peraza does not, which makes him a "utility infielder" in name only, no matter which half of that designation you focus on.

YEAR	TEAM	LVL	AGE	PA	DRC+	BABIP	BRR	FRAA	WARP
2018	CIN	MLB	24	683	101	.307	2.4	SS(156): -3.4, RF(1): -0.0	3.1
2019	CIN	MLB	25	403	78	.268	2.7	2B(78): 1.0, SS(39): 0.3, LF(33): -2.2	0.5
2020	BOS	MLB	26	120	93	.258	0.0	2B(27): 1.6, LF(5): -0.6, SS(3): -0.0	0.3
2021 FS	NYM	MLB	27	600	89	.297	1.3	2B 1, 3B -2	1.0
2021 DC	NYM	MLB	27	64	89	.297	0.1	2B 0, 3B 0	0.1

José Peraza, continued

Batted Ball Distribution

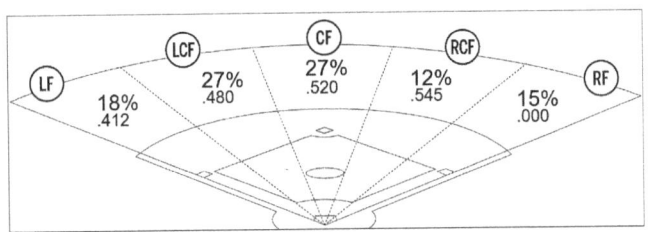

Strike Zone vs LHP

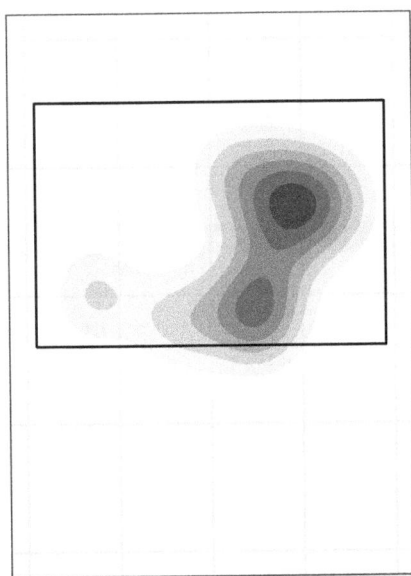

Strike Zone vs RHP

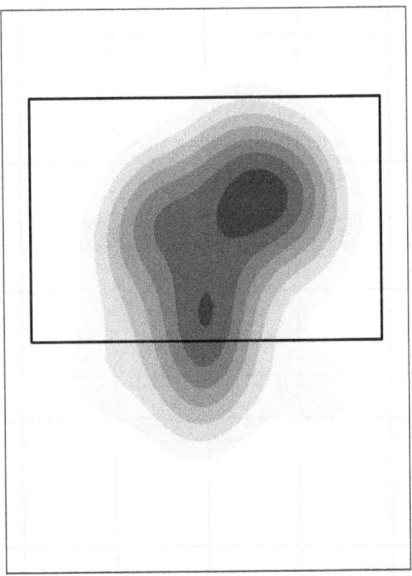

Type	Frequency	Velocity	H Movement	V Movement
● Fastball	100.0%	79.4 [58]	-8.3 [92]	-33.3 [49]

Dominic Smith 1B

Born: 06/15/95 Age: 26 Bats: L Throws: L
Height: 6'0" Weight: 239 Origin: Round 1, 2013 Draft (#11 overall)

YEAR	TEAM	LVL	AGE	PA	R	2B	3B	HR	RBI	BB	K	SB	CS	AVG/OBP/SLG
2018	LV	AAA	23	375	52	21	1	6	41	34	76	3	0	.258/.328/.380
2018	NYM	MLB	23	149	14	11	1	5	11	4	47	0	0	.224/.255/.420
2019	NYM	MLB	24	197	35	10	0	11	25	19	44	1	2	.282/.355/.525
2020	NYM	MLB	25	199	27	21	1	10	42	14	45	0	0	.316/.377/.616
2021 FS	NYM	MLB	26	600	80	31	1	23	88	47	146	0	1	.256/.324/.450
2021 DC	NYM	MLB	26	403	53	21	1	16	59	32	98	0	0	.256/.324/.450

Comparables: Tony Clark, Mike Jacobs, Carlos Delgado

Four years into his major-league career, Smith still hasn't eclipsed the 90-game mark in a season—though it's a good bet he would have given a standard-length 2020. Smith fought to establish himself as one of the best hitters in the National League while playing out of position, during a pandemic, with a compressed schedule, on a team that didn't truly support him when he took a knee for the national anthem during the Black Lives Matter protests. He stepped up as a leader as well, doing the hard work of following up a rare dismal offensive performance by holding court for an emotional press conference, explaining for reporters, teammates and the world just what the social justice movement is about for him. For a guy that couldn't seem to regularly crack a lineup until this year, it looks like Smith is just about everything you'd want in a ballplayer.

YEAR	TEAM	LVL	AGE	PA	DRC+	BABIP	BRR	FRAA	WARP
2018	LV	AAA	23	375	81	.315	1.9	1B(53): 6.5, LF(22): -0.2, RF(4): 2.2	0.5
2018	NYM	MLB	23	149	76	.297	0.3	1B(28): -0.5, LF(13): -1.9	-0.4
2019	NYM	MLB	24	197	111	.320	2.8	1B(36): -0.6, LF(32): -1.0, RF(1): -0.1	0.9
2020	NYM	MLB	25	199	120	.368	0.5	1B(25): -1.0, LF(23): -4.7	0.5
2021 FS	NYM	MLB	26	600	106	.311	-0.9	1B 1, LF -1	1.6
2021 DC	NYM	MLB	26	403	106	.311	-0.6	1B 1, LF 0	1.0

Dominic Smith, continued

Batted Ball Distribution

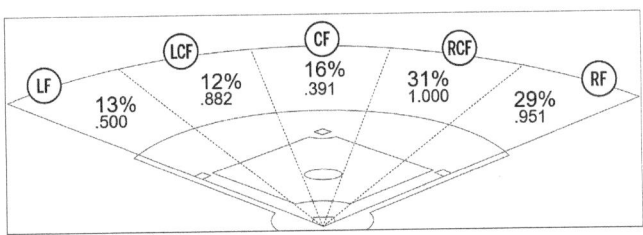

Strike Zone vs LHP   ### Strike Zone vs RHP

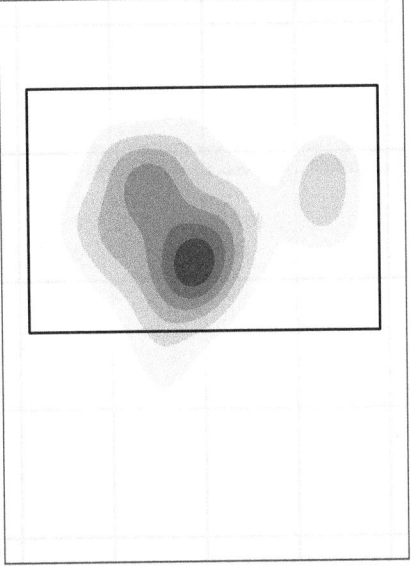

Jonathan Villar SS

Born: 05/02/91 Age: 30 Bats: S Throws: R
Height: 6'0" Weight: 233 Origin: International Free Agent, 2008

YEAR	TEAM	LVL	AGE	PA	R	2B	3B	HR	RBI	BB	K	SB	CS	AVG/OBP/SLG
2018	BAL	MLB	27	236	28	4	0	8	24	22	58	21	3	.258/.336/.392
2018	MIL	MLB	27	279	26	10	1	6	22	19	80	14	2	.261/.315/.377
2019	BAL	MLB	28	714	111	33	5	24	73	61	176	40	9	.274/.339/.453
2020	MIA	MLB	29	128	10	4	0	2	9	10	32	9	5	.259/.315/.345
2020	TOR	MLB	29	79	3	1	0	0	6	9	22	7	0	.188/.278/.203
2021 FS	NYM	MLB	30	600	62	21	2	15	64	56	168	37	11	.242/.317/.379
2021 DC	NYM	MLB	30	398	41	14	1	10	42	37	112	25	7	.242/.317/.379

Comparables: Jose Valentin, Alex Gonzalez, Dale Sveum

Acquired at the deadline to shore up the infield and add some baserunning ability, Villar's modest success as a Marlin did not carry over to the Jays. While he did manage to steal seven bases, making him the team leader in that regard, he struggled bitterly at the plate during his month with the team. It wasn't so much a change in his approach as that of his opponents: Pitchers fed him breaking pitches, and he flailed badly at them. His playing time dwindled in the last weeks of the season, and after being pinch-hit for in Game 1 of the Wild Card Series, the camera watched as Villar packed up his stuff and left, disappearing into the darkness of the clubhouse.

YEAR	TEAM	LVL	AGE	PA	DRC+	BABIP	BRR	FRAA	WARP
2018	BAL	MLB	27	236	84	.319	2.4	2B(36): 1.0, SS(18): 0.5	0.8
2018	MIL	MLB	27	279	81	.355	0.5	2B(74): -6.1	-0.3
2019	BAL	MLB	28	714	94	.341	5.6	2B(111): 4.0, SS(97): 0.9	3.3
2020	MIA	MLB	29	128	63	.337	-1.4	SS(14): -3.5, 2B(12): -0.5, CF(2): -0.2	-0.8
2020	TOR	MLB	29	79	62	.271	0.6	2B(13): 1.7, SS(7): 0.1	0.1
2021 FS	NYM	MLB	30	600	91	.323	2.9	2B 0, CF -2	1.2
2021 DC	NYM	MLB	30	398	91	.323	1.9	2B 0, CF -1	0.8

Jonathan Villar, continued

Batted Ball Distribution

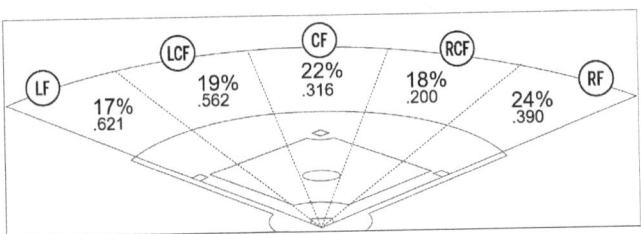

Strike Zone vs LHP **Strike Zone vs RHP**

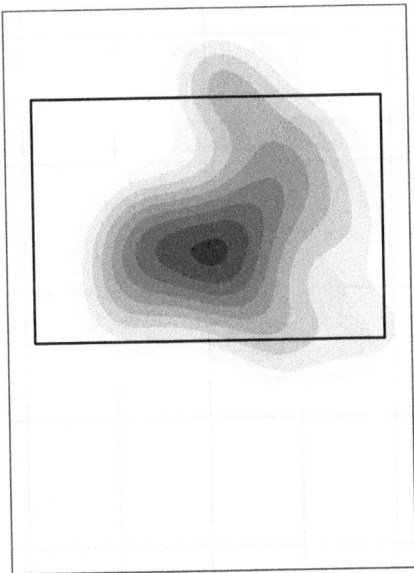
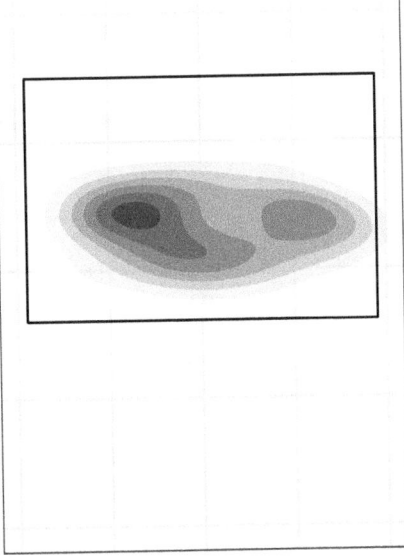

Jacob Barnes RHP

Born: 04/14/90 Age: 31 Bats: R Throws: R
Height: 6'2" Weight: 231 Origin: Round 14, 2011 Draft (#431 overall)

YEAR	TEAM	LVL	AGE	W	L	SV	G	GS	IP	H	HR	BB/9	K/9	K	GB%	BABIP
2018	RMV	AAA	28	1	0	2	11	0	11^2	5	0	6.2	7.7	10	58.1%	.167
2018	MIL	MLB	28	0	1	2	49	0	48^2	51	4	4.3	8.7	47	49.0%	.331
2019	SA	AAA	29	2	0	1	14	0	14	14	3	1.3	9.6	15	50.0%	.282
2019	KC	MLB	29	0	4	0	15	0	13	14	4	7.6	6.9	10	50.0%	.250
2019	MIL	MLB	29	1	1	0	18	1	19^2	22	3	5.0	10.1	22	46.8%	.322
2020	LAA	MLB	30	0	2	0	18	0	18	19	1	2.0	12.0	24	39.6%	.391
2021 FS	NYM	MLB	31	2	2	0	57	0	50	44	6	3.9	9.7	53	46.5%	.292
2021 DC	NYM	MLB	31	1	1	0	22	0	17.3	15	2	3.9	9.7	18	46.5%	.292

Comparables: Kelvin Herrera, Hunter Strickland, Paul Sewald

Occasionally, diagnosing the source of a pitcher's woes are easy: No need to get Freudian or Jungian when you can break out the velocity charts. These ink blots are clearer, but wringing solutions from them is rarely simple when *pitch harder* is as unhelpful a refrain as *be happier* is in a different sort of analysis. Barnes enlisted self-help as best he could and restored some of his velocity and results in 2020, but only enough to be cut from one team instead of two. Now, he'll try to achieve inner peace with the Mets.

YEAR	TEAM	LVL	AGE	WHIP	ERA	DRA-	WARP	MPH	FB%	WHF	CSP
2018	RMV	AAA	28	1.11	1.54	89	0.1				
2018	MIL	MLB	28	1.52	3.33	78	0.8	97.4	50.5%	30.1%	
2019	SA	AAA	29	1.14	4.50	60	0.4				
2019	KC	MLB	29	1.92	8.31	147	-0.3	96.1	50.4%	25.2%	
2019	MIL	MLB	29	1.68	6.86	113	0.0	95.3	46.4%	21.8%	
2020	LAA	MLB	30	1.28	5.50	73	0.4	97.3	46.6%	34.2%	
2021 FS	NYM	MLB	31	1.31	3.79	87	0.6	96.6	48.3%	28.4%	42.6%
2021 DC	NYM	MLB	31	1.31	3.79	87	0.2	96.6	48.3%	28.4%	42.6%

Jacob Barnes, continued

Pitch Shape vs LHH

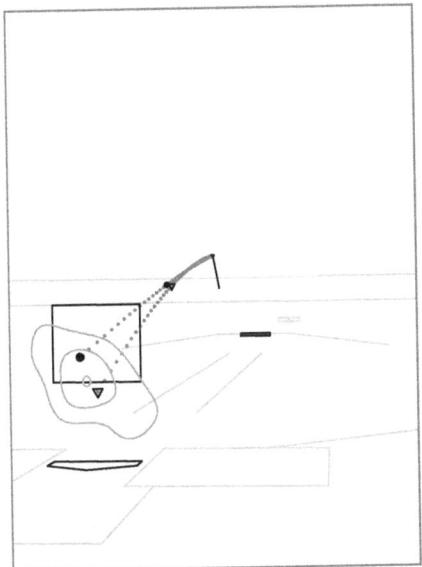

Pitch Shape vs RHH

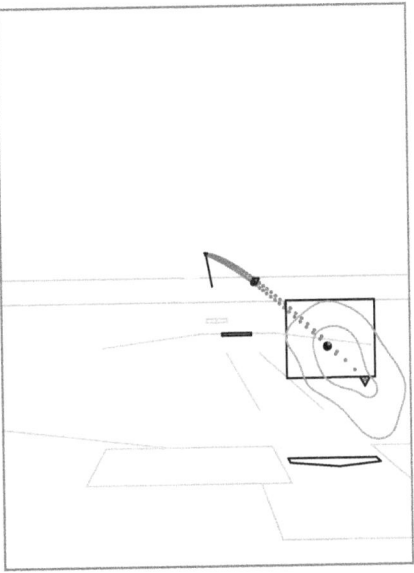

Type	Frequency	Velocity	H Movement	V Movement
● Fastball	46.6%	95.3 [109]	-2.9 [118]	-10.6 [113]
▽ Slider	52.4%	89.6 [125]	4.2 [96]	-24.1 [128]

Dellin Betances RHP

Born: 03/23/88 Age: 33 Bats: R Throws: R
Height: 6'8" Weight: 265 Origin: Round 8, 2006 Draft (#254 overall)

YEAR	TEAM	LVL	AGE	W	L	SV	G	GS	IP	H	HR	BB/9	K/9	K	GB%	BABIP
2018	NYY	MLB	30	4	6	4	66	0	66^2	44	7	3.5	15.5	115	43.7%	.319
2019	NYY	MLB	31	0	0	0	1	0	0^2	0	0	0.0	27.0	2		
2020	NYM	MLB	32	0	1	0	15	0	11^2	12	0	9.3	8.5	11	41.2%	.353
2021 FS	NYM	MLB	33	2	2	0	57	0	50	40	5	5.5	12.0	66	44.4%	.306
2021 DC	NYM	MLB	33	2	2	0	45	0	52.3	42	5	5.5	12.0	69	44.4%	.306

Comparables: Craig Kimbrel, Kenley Jansen, Brad Lidge

The Mets' biggest free agent pitching acquisition prior to the 2020 season ended up as a pretty good avatar for the way many of us experienced this past calendar year. After all, Betances' season was littered with health scares, possessed of several false starts, and punctuated by moments of abysmal failure. Even his celebrated fastball did an effective impression of time during quarantine by crawling to a standstill. After picking up his pricey $6.8 million player option, he and the Mets will both hope to turn the page on a remarkably bad year by healing up and starting over. Like many people, he'll hope to go back to the way things were, in 2021, but he may not be able to do so

YEAR	TEAM	LVL	AGE	WHIP	ERA	DRA-	WARP	MPH	FB%	WHF	CSP
2018	NYY	MLB	30	1.05	2.70	48	2.1	99.7	47.8%	37.4%	
2019	NYY	MLB	31	0.00	0.00	208	0.0	95.3	62.5%	0.0%	
2020	NYM	MLB	32	2.06	7.71	108	0.1	95.8	49.0%	21.4%	
2021 FS	NYM	MLB	33	1.43	4.18	92	0.5	98.2	48.4%	30.9%	46.5%
2021 DC	NYM	MLB	33	1.43	4.18	92	0.5	98.2	48.4%	30.9%	46.5%

Dellin Betances, continued

Pitch Shape vs LHH

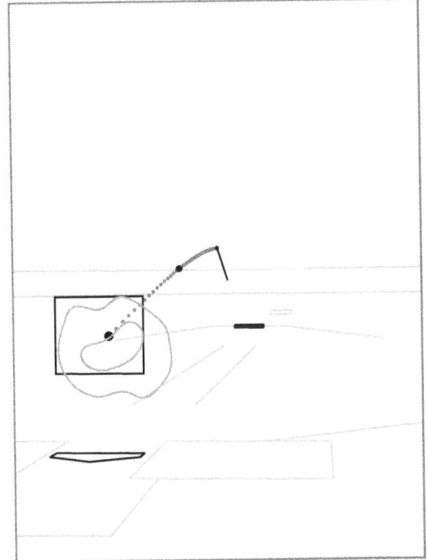

Pitch Shape vs RHH

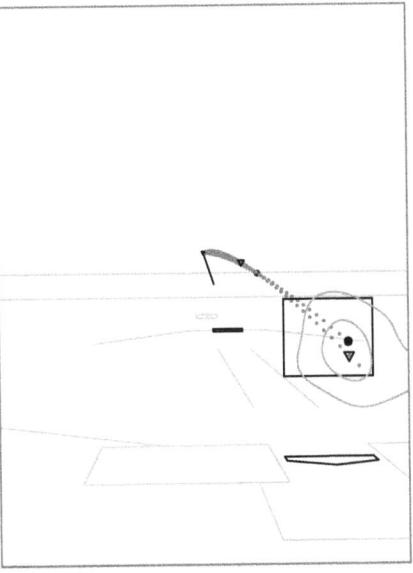

Type	Frequency	Velocity	H Movement	V Movement
● Fastball	45.6%	93.7 [104]	-2.9 [118]	-17.6 [93]
+ Cutter	3.3%	95.1 [143]	-2.6 [71]	-16.8 [129]
▽ Slider	39.8%	82.8 [95]	10.2 [119]	-35.7 [94]
◇ Curveball	11.2%	86.1 [129]	6.3 [95]	-40.3 [118]

Brad Brach RHP

Born: 04/12/86   Age: 35   Bats: R   Throws: R
Height: 6'6"   Weight: 215   Origin: Round 42, 2008 Draft (#1275 overall)

YEAR	TEAM	LVL	AGE	W	L	SV	G	GS	IP	H	HR	BB/9	K/9	K	GB%	BABIP
2018	ATL	MLB	32	1	2	1	27	0	23^2	22	1	3.4	8.4	22	45.8%	.296
2018	BAL	MLB	32	1	2	11	42	0	39	50	4	4.4	8.8	38	46.9%	.374
2019	NYM	MLB	33	1	1	0	16	0	14^2	15	1	1.8	9.2	15	34.9%	.341
2019	CHC	MLB	33	4	3	0	42	0	39^2	42	3	6.4	10.2	45	39.3%	.375
2020	NYM	MLB	34	1	0	0	14	0	12^1	8	2	10.2	10.2	14	34.5%	.222
2021 FS	NYM	MLB	35	2	2	0	57	0	50	45	7	4.8	9.1	50	40.2%	.290
2021 DC	NYM	MLB	35	2	2	0	51	0	11.3	10	1	4.8	9.1	11	40.2%	.290

Comparables: Steve Cishek, Tyler Clippard, Brian Fuentes

Credit Brach with trying to make the best of a bad situation over 12 ⅓ miserable innings. Just two years removed from his peak with Baltimore, he's shifted from "wildly underrated" to just plain wild, as he now has to focus on keeping hitters from squaring up his diminished fastball. He's moved to relying on his cutter more frequently, but take a look at that stat line and let us know if it helped. Even when he could locate the erratic pitch, opposing hitters pounced on it for a .583 slugging percentage. At this point, he might be more of a righty specialist, and that makes him more of a sixth-inning situational arm than the slick setup man he once was.

YEAR	TEAM	LVL	AGE	WHIP	ERA	DRA-	WARP	MPH	FB%	WHF	CSP
2018	ATL	MLB	32	1.31	1.52	75	0.4	96.0	52.3%	28.6%	
2018	BAL	MLB	32	1.77	4.85	95	0.3	95.4	61.4%	29.5%	
2019	NYM	MLB	33	1.23	3.68	77	0.2	95.4	71.0%	26.4%	
2019	CHC	MLB	33	1.76	6.13	109	0.0	95.7	60.5%	27.5%	
2020	NYM	MLB	34	1.78	5.84	131	-0.1	91.8	68.7%	31.9%	
2021 FS	NYM	MLB	35	1.45	4.50	99	0.3	94.8	62.5%	28.7%	44.1%
2021 DC	NYM	MLB	35	1.45	4.50	99	0.1	94.8	62.5%	28.7%	44.1%

Brad Brach, continued

Pitch Shape vs LHH

Pitch Shape vs RHH

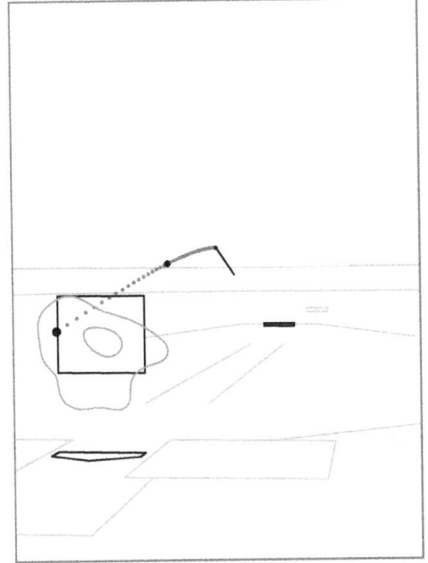
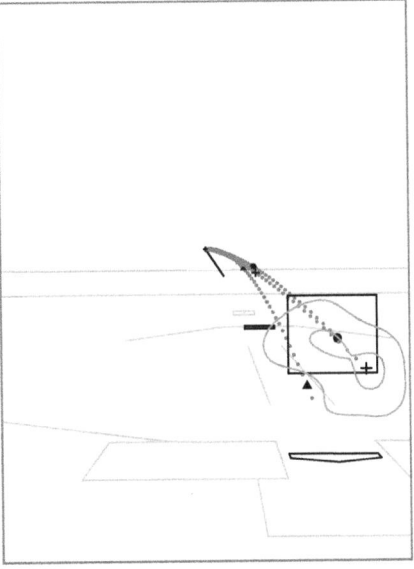

Type	Frequency	Velocity	H Movement	V Movement
● Fastball	36.1%	90.5 [93]	-7.2 [97]	-17.8 [93]
+ Cutter	31.8%	87.2 [93]	2.4 [103]	-22.9 [105]
▲ Changeup	23.5%	83.4 [93]	-12.7 [95]	-35.4 [78]
▽ Slider	7.5%	81.3 [88]	6.7 [106]	-36.6 [92]

Carlos Carrasco RHP

Born: 03/21/87 Age: 34 Bats: R Throws: R
Height: 6'4" Weight: 224 Origin: International Free Agent, 2003

YEAR	TEAM	LVL	AGE	W	L	SV	G	GS	IP	H	HR	BB/9	K/9	K	GB%	BABIP
2018	CLE	MLB	31	17	10	0	32	30	192	173	21	2.0	10.8	231	47.2%	.317
2019	CLE	MLB	32	6	7	1	23	12	80	92	18	1.8	10.8	96	41.0%	.357
2020	CLE	MLB	33	3	4	0	12	12	68	55	8	3.6	10.9	82	46.2%	.294
2021 FS	NYM	MLB	34	10	7	0	26	26	150	131	21	2.6	10.5	175	45.2%	.296
2021 DC	NYM	MLB	34	10	7	0	27	27	156.7	137	22	2.6	10.5	183	45.2%	.296

Comparables: Corey Kluber, Zack Greinke, Johnny Cueto

A year after being diagnosed with leukemia, Carrasco took every turn in the rotation until it was time to rest for the final weekend ahead of the playoffs—and he did so with aplomb. He made a few tweaks along the way: leaning on his changeup at a career-high rate, and swapping his sinker for a curveball. Other than a few more walks, the results were as good as we've come to expect. Any scenario that saw Carrasco making a full return would've been heartening, but this one seems particularly so. Good on you, Cookie.

YEAR	TEAM	LVL	AGE	WHIP	ERA	DRA-	WARP	MPH	FB%	WHF	CSP
2018	CLE	MLB	31	1.12	3.38	65	5.3	95.6	44.9%	33.5%	
2019	CLE	MLB	32	1.35	5.29	111	0.2	95.6	46.0%	31.2%	
2020	CLE	MLB	33	1.21	2.91	81	1.3	95.6	39.6%	32.7%	
2021 FS	NYM	MLB	34	1.17	3.37	80	3.1	95.6	43.2%	32.6%	45.6%
2021 DC	NYM	MLB	34	1.17	3.37	80	3.2	95.6	43.2%	32.6%	45.6%

Carlos Carrasco, continued

Pitch Shape vs LHH

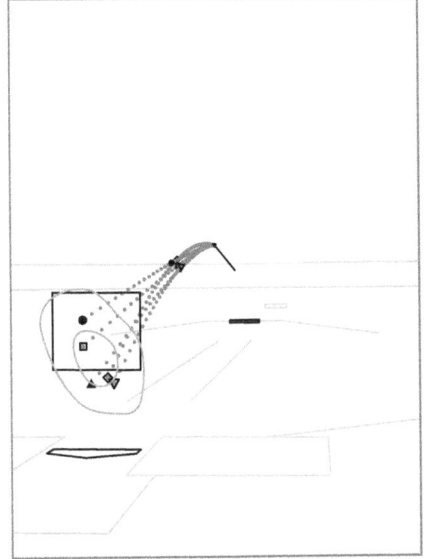

Pitch Shape vs RHH

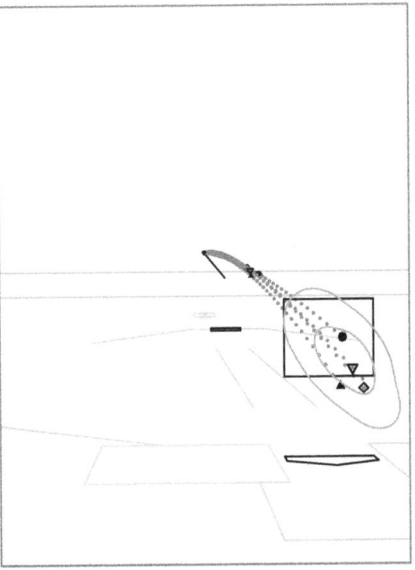

Type	Frequency	Velocity	H Movement	V Movement
● Fastball	34.4%	93.9 [104]	-7.9 [94]	-14.2 [103]
□ Sinker	4.9%	92.5 [100]	-14 [93]	-21.4 [97]
▲ Changeup	27.1%	87.8 [110]	-6.2 [129]	-29.8 [94]
▽ Slider	21.3%	86.6 [112]	2.7 [91]	-30.8 [109]
◇ Curveball	12.0%	83.9 [120]	7.3 [99]	-39.8 [119]

Miguel Castro RHP

Born: 12/24/94   Age: 26   Bats: R   Throws: R
Height: 6'7"   Weight: 205   Origin: International Free Agent, 2012

YEAR	TEAM	LVL	AGE	W	L	SV	G	GS	IP	H	HR	BB/9	K/9	K	GB%	BABIP
2018	BAL	MLB	23	2	7	0	63	1	86^1	75	9	5.2	5.9	57	48.5%	.259
2019	BAL	MLB	24	1	3	2	65	0	73^1	63	10	5.0	8.7	71	48.3%	.269
2020	NYM	MLB	25	2	2	1	26	0	24^2	28	4	4.7	13.9	38	52.4%	.407
2021 FS	NYM	MLB	26	2	2	0	57	0	50	45	6	4.8	9.7	53	47.3%	.295
2021 DC	NYM	MLB	26	2	2	0	45	0	40.7	36	5	4.8	9.7	43	47.3%	.295

Comparables: Ryan Perry, Ed Nunez, Dave Beard

Little changed in his peripherals, but the start of his age-25 season looked to be something of a long-awaited coming out party for Castro. Since his teens, he had the raw heat on his fastball to be an oohs-and-ahs relief prospect, but his gangly mechanics commonly resulted in too many free passes. With only a brief uptick in velocity on his secondaries and a slight rise in whiff rate, Castro strung together 15 glorious innings of strikeout after strikeout, punctuated by far fewer free passes. The magic wore off after his midseason trade to the Mets, but he remains tantalizing due to his high-end velocity and the possibility that, for a few weeks at a time, at least, he can smooth things out enough to be a force in the middle innings.

YEAR	TEAM	LVL	AGE	WHIP	ERA	DRA-	WARP	MPH	FB%	WHF	CSP
2018	BAL	MLB	23	1.45	3.96	145	-1.5	98.3	58.1%	23.6%	
2019	BAL	MLB	24	1.42	4.66	82	1.1	99.0	49.1%	27.6%	
2020	NYM	MLB	25	1.66	4.01	68	0.6	99.8	50.7%	30.9%	
2021 FS	NYM	MLB	26	1.44	4.42	98	0.3	99.0	52.0%	27.4%	46.6%
2021 DC	NYM	MLB	26	1.44	4.42	98	0.2	99.0	52.0%	27.4%	46.6%

Miguel Castro, continued

Pitch Shape vs LHH

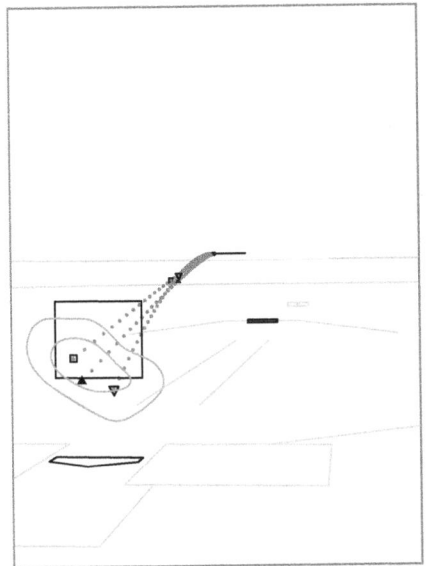

Pitch Shape vs RHH

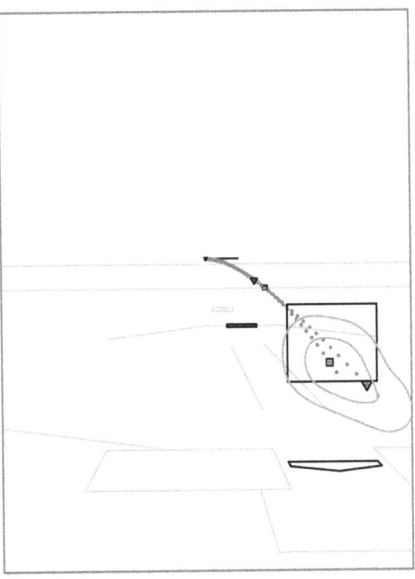

Type	Frequency	Velocity	H Movement	V Movement
☐ Sinker	50.7%	98.1 [129]	-15.9 [79]	-19.1 [105]
▲ Changeup	17.6%	92.4 [128]	-16.8 [73]	-26 [104]
▽ Slider	31.7%	87 [113]	5.8 [102]	-30.7 [109]

Jacob deGrom RHP

Born: 06/19/88 Age: 33 Bats: L Throws: R
Height: 6'4" Weight: 180 Origin: Round 9, 2010 Draft (#272 overall)

YEAR	TEAM	LVL	AGE	W	L	SV	G	GS	IP	H	HR	BB/9	K/9	K	GB%	BABIP
2018	NYM	MLB	30	10	9	0	32	32	217	152	10	1.9	11.2	269	46.2%	.283
2019	NYM	MLB	31	11	8	0	32	32	204	154	19	1.9	11.2	254	43.6%	.284
2020	NYM	MLB	32	4	2	0	12	12	68	47	7	2.4	13.8	104	42.5%	.288
2021 FS	NYM	MLB	33	11	6	0	26	26	150	117	16	2.2	11.9	197	43.4%	.295
2021 DC	NYM	MLB	33	12	6	0	29	29	174.7	136	19	2.2	11.9	230	43.4%	.295

Comparables: Corey Kluber, Kenta Maeda, Max Scherzer

Few pitchers continue to add velocity in their early 30s, but BP's Rob Arthur discovered that deGrom truly is in a class of his own: Only two starting pitchers since 2008 have added as much oomph to their fastball during the middle of their career, and both of those pitchers were injury-riddled hurlers, not an established star like deGrom. He's now the hardest-throwing starter in baseball over the age of 30, and he's complemented that by becoming more unpredictable in his pitch selection, often working his devastating slider out of the zone in hitters' counts instead of leaning into his heater. So even though the shortened season saw him down to a mere Cy Young finalist rather than Cy Young winner, there's reason to believe that deGrom will extend his peak even once his fastball velocity inevitably plateaus.

YEAR	TEAM	LVL	AGE	WHIP	ERA	DRA-	WARP	MPH	FB%	WHF	CSP
2018	NYM	MLB	30	0.91	1.70	46	8.0	98.2	52.1%	31.5%	
2019	NYM	MLB	31	0.97	2.43	46	7.8	98.8	49.3%	31.9%	
2020	NYM	MLB	32	0.96	2.38	57	2.2	100.3	44.9%	41.0%	
2021 FS	NYM	MLB	33	1.03	2.38	59	4.9	99.0	48.8%	34.2%	46.2%
2021 DC	NYM	MLB	33	1.03	2.38	59	5.7	99.0	48.8%	34.2%	46.2%

Jacob deGrom, continued

Pitch Shape vs LHH

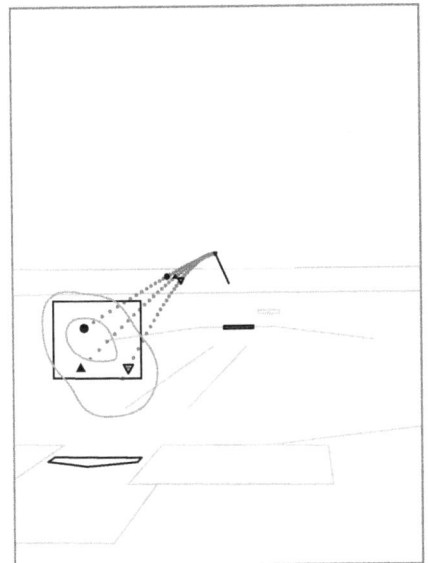

Pitch Shape vs RHH

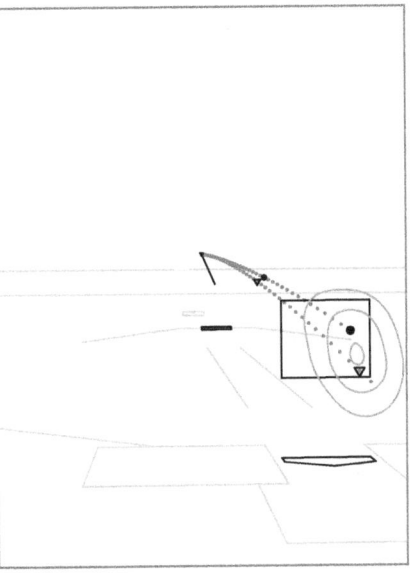

Type	Frequency	Velocity	H Movement	V Movement
● Fastball	44.8%	98.7 [120]	-6.1 [103]	-10.3 [114]
▲ Changeup	16.9%	91.6 [125]	-12 [99]	-25.9 [104]
▽ Slider	35.6%	92.7 [139]	3.4 [93]	-23.9 [128]

Edwin Díaz RHP

Born: 03/22/94 Age: 27 Bats: R Throws: R
Height: 6'3" Weight: 165 Origin: Round 3, 2012 Draft (#98 overall)

YEAR	TEAM	LVL	AGE	W	L	SV	G	GS	IP	H	HR	BB/9	K/9	K	GB%	BABIP
2018	SEA	MLB	24	0	4	57	73	0	73^1	41	5	2.1	15.2	124	46.6%	.281
2019	NYM	MLB	25	2	7	26	66	0	58	58	15	3.4	15.4	99	36.4%	.381
2020	NYM	MLB	26	2	1	6	26	0	25^2	18	2	4.9	17.5	50	45.5%	.381
2021 FS	NYM	MLB	27	3	2	36	57	0	50	35	5	3.6	14.5	80	40.8%	.311
2021 DC	NYM	MLB	27	2	2	36	51	0	52.3	36	5	3.6	14.5	84	40.8%	.311

Comparables: José Leclerc, Michael Feliz, Francisco Rodríguez

It took until September of his second season with the Mets, but Díaz is finally starting to resemble the pitcher the team thought they were acquiring in their blockbuster trade, instead of the combustible reliever they received in 2019. The signs that his first season in Queens could have been a fluke were always there, but after being gently worked back into high-leverage situations, Díaz turned up the heat and struck out 45.5 percent of the batters he faced in 2020. He ended his season with a dominant stretch that reaffirmed his grasp on the closer role and as the anchor of the bullpen.

YEAR	TEAM	LVL	AGE	WHIP	ERA	DRA-	WARP	MPH	FB%	WHF	CSP
2018	SEA	MLB	24	0.79	1.96	39	2.7	99.3	62.5%	39.8%	
2019	NYM	MLB	25	1.38	5.59	60	1.5	99.6	66.1%	37.9%	
2020	NYM	MLB	26	1.25	1.75	45	1.0	99.6	61.9%	48.2%	
2021 FS	NYM	MLB	27	1.10	2.66	63	1.3	99.5	63.9%	41.5%	46.3%
2021 DC	NYM	MLB	27	1.10	2.66	63	1.3	99.5	63.9%	41.5%	46.3%

Edwin Díaz, continued

Pitch Shape vs LHH

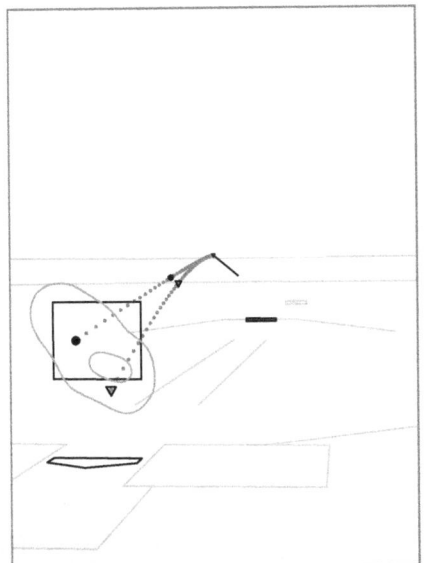

Pitch Shape vs RHH

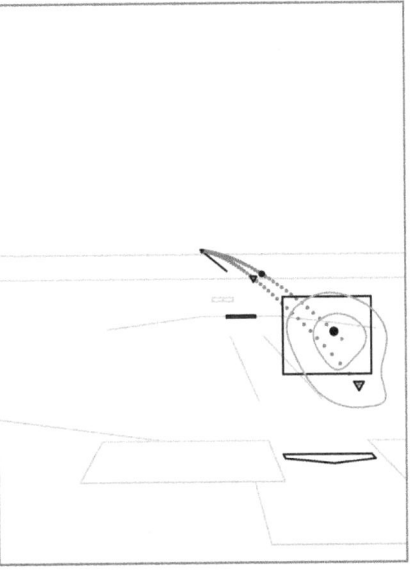

Type	Frequency	Velocity	H Movement	V Movement
● Fastball	61.5%	98 [117]	-12.8 [71]	-14 [103]
▽ Slider	37.9%	89.8 [126]	1.1 [84]	-26.2 [122]

Mets Player Analysis - 63

Jeurys Familia   RHP
Born: 10/10/89   Age: 31   Bats: R   Throws: R
Height: 6'3"   Weight: 240   Origin: International Free Agent, 2007

YEAR	TEAM	LVL	AGE	W	L	SV	G	GS	IP	H	HR	BB/9	K/9	K	GB%	BABIP
2018	OAK	MLB	28	4	2	1	30	0	31^1	24	2	4.0	11.5	40	40.3%	.293
2018	NYM	MLB	28	4	4	17	40	0	40^2	36	1	3.1	9.5	43	50.9%	.315
2019	NYM	MLB	29	4	2	0	66	0	60	62	7	6.3	9.4	63	50.0%	.350
2020	NYM	MLB	30	2	0	0	25	0	26^2	20	2	6.4	7.8	23	60.0%	.247
2021 FS	NYM	MLB	31	2	2	0	57	0	50	45	5	5.2	9.2	51	53.1%	.297
2021 DC	NYM	MLB	31	2	2	0	51	0	52.3	47	5	5.2	9.2	53	53.1%	.297

Comparables: Kelvin Herrera, Mychal Givens, Randy Myers

There were a few hints that the stalwart of the Mets' bullpen might be rounding into form during the abbreviated 2020 season: He started strong in July, and his velocity improved as the short season wore on, but by the end of the year it seemed clear that 2019 wasn't just a fluke. Familia couldn't translate the improved giddyup on his sinker and slider into whiffs, instead working to keep the ball in the infield. Back when he was a top-flight reliever, Familia could do both: induce grounders but also punch hitters out with regularity. In his present form, he's more of a fringy setup option; though the uniform remains the same, he's a different pitcher than in his prime.

YEAR	TEAM	LVL	AGE	WHIP	ERA	DRA-	WARP	MPH	FB%	WHF	CSP
2018	OAK	MLB	28	1.21	3.45	68	0.7	98.5	66.8%	35.4%	
2018	NYM	MLB	28	1.23	2.88	103	0.1	97.8	70.2%	26.7%	
2019	NYM	MLB	29	1.73	5.70	120	-0.3	97.8	65.8%	28.6%	
2020	NYM	MLB	30	1.46	3.71	90	0.4	98.5	59.7%	27.8%	
2021 FS	NYM	MLB	31	1.48	4.40	97	0.3	98.1	64.7%	28.9%	47.2%
2021 DC	NYM	MLB	31	1.48	4.40	97	0.3	98.1	64.7%	28.9%	47.2%

Jeurys Familia, continued

Pitch Shape vs LHH

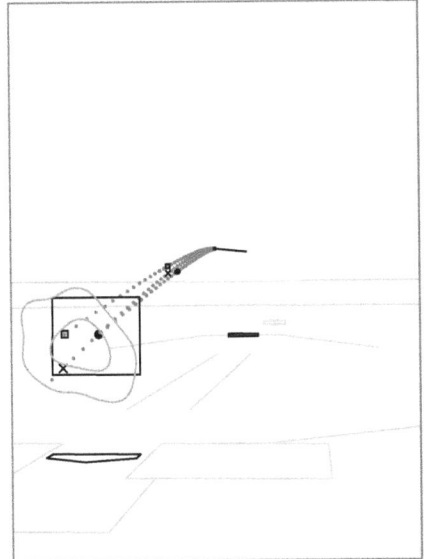

Pitch Shape vs RHH

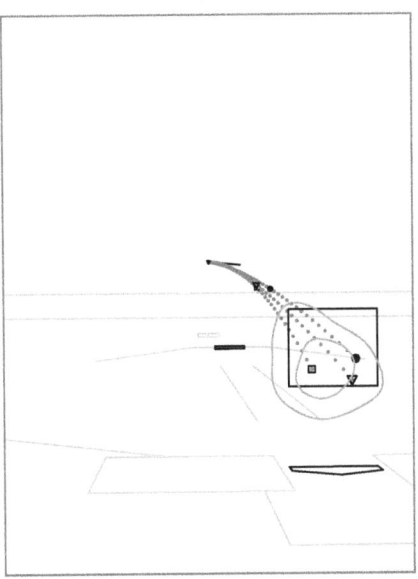

Type	Frequency	Velocity	H Movement	V Movement
● Fastball	14.0%	97.4 [115]	-10.2 [83]	-13.6 [104]
□ Sinker	44.5%	96.6 [122]	-15.7 [81]	-21.9 [95]
✕ Splitter	11.0%	91.2 [127]	-11.7 [86]	-26.9 [108]
▽ Slider	28.5%	89.8 [126]	-0.6 [78]	-24.1 [128]

Robert Gsellman RHP

Born: 07/18/93 Age: 27 Bats: R Throws: R
Height: 6'4" Weight: 200 Origin: Round 13, 2011 Draft (#402 overall)

YEAR	TEAM	LVL	AGE	W	L	SV	G	GS	IP	H	HR	BB/9	K/9	K	GB%	BABIP
2018	NYM	MLB	24	6	3	13	68	0	80	76	8	3.1	7.9	70	50.4%	.294
2019	NYM	MLB	25	2	3	1	52	0	63^2	64	7	3.3	8.5	60	43.6%	.317
2020	NYM	MLB	26	0	0	0	6	4	14	22	4	5.1	5.8	9	41.5%	.367
2021 FS	NYM	MLB	27	2	2	0	57	0	50	50	7	3.5	7.7	42	45.5%	.294
2021 DC	NYM	MLB	27	6	4	0	44	6	66.3	66	10	3.5	7.7	57	45.5%	.294

Comparables: Reynaldo López, Chase De Jong, Joe Ross

Gsellman's 2020 had more false starts than an elementary school track meet. First a triceps injury set his debut back, then he had just one appearance in the bullpen before getting shifted into the starting rotation. That went just about as badly as it could have; he exceeded two innings as a starter just once, and not because he was designed to be an opener. After one final bullpen appearance, he hit the injured list again, this time with a fractured rib, and his season was over. It's hard to be surprised at the terrible stat line, given his medical issues and the surprise shift in role mid-season, but Gsellman should be counted on to return to his role as a sixth- or seventh-inning relief arm, not as a swingman or back-end starter. Despite his wide assortment of pitches and prospect pedigree, he's best served in a mid-leverage relief role without being asked to do much more.

YEAR	TEAM	LVL	AGE	WHIP	ERA	DRA-	WARP	MPH	FB%	WHF	CSP
2018	NYM	MLB	24	1.30	4.28	97	0.5	96.1	62.8%	22.4%	
2019	NYM	MLB	25	1.37	4.66	99	0.3	97.1	51.8%	26.4%	
2020	NYM	MLB	26	2.14	9.64	130	-0.1	95.8	64.0%	16.9%	
2021 FS	NYM	MLB	27	1.39	4.62	104	0.1	96.6	57.5%	23.4%	47.5%
2021 DC	NYM	MLB	27	1.39	4.62	104	0.3	96.6	57.5%	23.4%	47.5%

Robert Gsellman, continued

Pitch Shape vs LHH

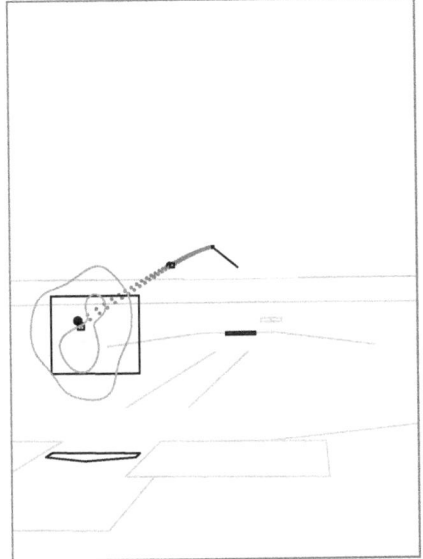

Pitch Shape vs RHH

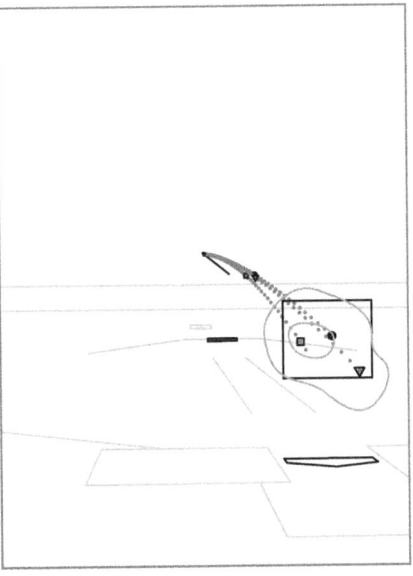

Type	Frequency	Velocity	H Movement	V Movement
● Fastball	29.3%	94.1 [105]	-8.7 [90]	-13.3 [105]
□ Sinker	34.4%	93.5 [106]	-12.1 [107]	-16 [115]
▲ Changeup	7.2%	86.1 [104]	-12.4 [97]	-24.8 [107]
▽ Slider	21.7%	89.6 [125]	-0.3 [79]	-23.6 [129]
◇ Curveball	6.9%	79.5 [103]	9.4 [107]	-49.3 [98]

Jared Hughes RHP
Born: 07/04/85   Age: 36   Bats: R   Throws: R
Height: 6'7"   Weight: 240   Origin: Round 4, 2006 Draft (#110 overall)

YEAR	TEAM	LVL	AGE	W	L	SV	G	GS	IP	H	HR	BB/9	K/9	K	GB%	BABIP
2018	CIN	MLB	32	4	3	7	72	0	78^2	57	4	2.6	6.8	59	63.6%	.254
2019	CIN	MLB	33	3	4	1	47	0	48^1	41	6	3.5	6.3	34	59.7%	.259
2019	PHI	MLB	33	2	1	0	25	0	23	16	7	3.1	7.8	20	53.2%	.167
2020	NYM	MLB	34	1	2	0	18	0	22^1	23	3	5.6	8.5	21	56.5%	.303
2021 FS	NYM	MLB	35	2	2	0	57	0	50	47	6	3.8	7.2	40	57.7%	.285

Comparables: Javy Guerra, Javier López, Cory Gearrin

Five unearned runs made Hughes' first (and likely last) season in New York look more palatable than his ERA would suggest. His velocity never rebounded to where it was prior to 2019, so his ceiling is probably now that of a league-average reliever.

YEAR	TEAM	LVL	AGE	WHIP	ERA	DRA-	WARP	MPH	FB%	WHF	CSP
2018	CIN	MLB	32	1.02	1.94	102	0.3	93.5	86.0%	25.4%	
2019	CIN	MLB	33	1.24	4.10	94	0.4	92.9	81.1%	22.1%	
2019	PHI	MLB	33	1.04	3.91	94	0.2	93.1	79.9%	24.0%	
2020	NYM	MLB	34	1.66	4.84	95	0.3	93.3	59.4%	32.3%	
2021 FS	NYM	MLB	35	1.38	4.31	98	0.3	93.2	76.2%	26.0%	39.6%

Jared Hughes, continued

Pitch Shape vs LHH

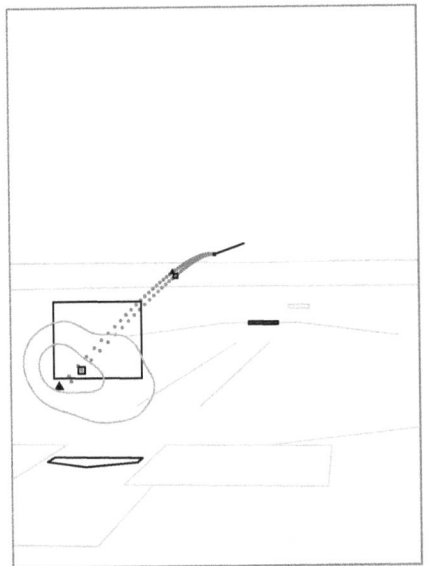

Pitch Shape vs RHH

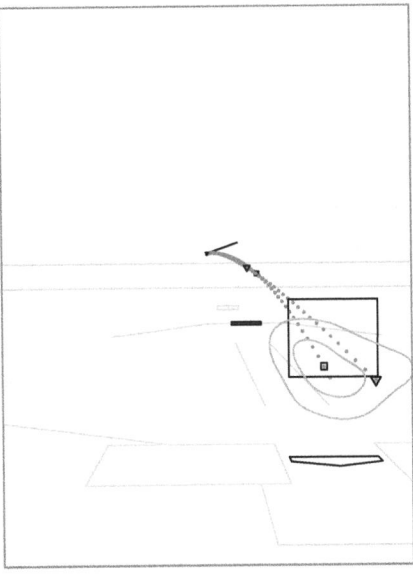

Type	Frequency	Velocity	H Movement	V Movement
● Fastball	7.2%	92.3 [99]	-7.7 [95]	-20.3 [86]
☐ Sinker	51.3%	91.5 [95]	-13.8 [95]	-30.2 [69]
▲ Changeup	13.7%	84.4 [97]	-8.2 [118]	-33.6 [83]
▽ Slider	26.4%	81 [87]	11.9 [125]	-34 [99]

Tommy Hunter RHP

Born: 07/03/86 Age: 35 Bats: R Throws: R
Height: 6'3" Weight: 250 Origin: Round 1, 2007 Draft (#54 overall)

YEAR	TEAM	LVL	AGE	W	L	SV	G	GS	IP	H	HR	BB/9	K/9	K	GB%	BABIP
2018	PHI	MLB	31	5	4	4	65	0	64	65	6	2.1	7.2	51	50.7%	.304
2019	PHI	MLB	32	0	0	0	5	0	5^1	2	0	0.0	8.4	5	30.8%	.154
2020	PHI	MLB	33	0	1	1	24	0	24^2	22	2	2.2	9.1	25	41.2%	.308
2021 FS	*NYM*	*MLB*	*34*	*2*	*2*	*0*	*57*	*0*	*50*	*47*	*6*	*2.3*	*8.4*	*46*	*45.1%*	*.290*

Comparables: Anthony Swarzak, Glen Perkins, Casey Janssen

Hunter's most memorable moment of the 2020 season was a press conference in late August, when criticism of the Phillies bullpen had reached its peak. Hunter, sick of the comments and flexing his biceps, lamented that "baseball is so messed up," and assured people that Phillies' pitchers were "giving everything we have." It was a big moment, and narratively, a potential turnaround for the bullpen and Hunter specifically, who was in a stretch of eight scoreless starts. Unfortunately, the lively presser didn't do much for his on-field work, as Hunter wound up with a 10.33 ERA with RISP, as batters hit .304 against him at Citizens Bank Park. Hunter has always been capable of spurts of shutdown success—but rarely more than that, and the shortened season did not allow him room to schedule many.

YEAR	TEAM	LVL	AGE	WHIP	ERA	DRA-	WARP	MPH	FB%	WHF	CSP
2018	PHI	MLB	31	1.25	3.80	101	0.3	97.2	86.0%	21.2%	
2019	PHI	MLB	32	0.38	0.00	105	0.0	95.1	86.1%	28.1%	
2020	PHI	MLB	33	1.14	4.01	81	0.5	94.0	76.8%	25.7%	
2021 FS	*NYM*	*MLB*	*34*	*1.20*	*3.51*	*85*	*0.6*	*95.4*	*81.2%*	*24.0%*	*45.8%*

Tommy Hunter, continued

Pitch Shape vs LHH

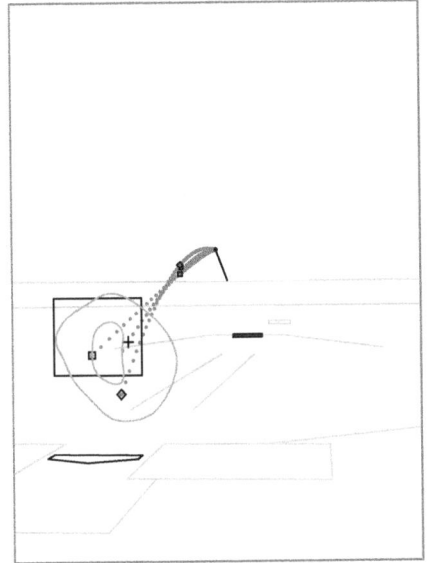

Pitch Shape vs RHH

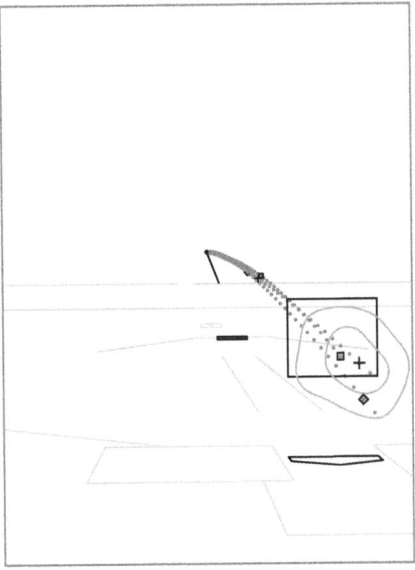

Type	Frequency	Velocity	H Movement	V Movement
☐ Sinker	41.2%	92.8 [102]	-12.2 [107]	-18.1 [108]
+ Cutter	33.9%	90.6 [114]	3.1 [108]	-20.3 [115]
◇ Curveball	23.2%	82.5 [115]	11.7 [117]	-41.4 [116]

Franklyn Kilome RHP

Born: 06/25/95 Age: 26 Bats: R Throws: R
Height: 6'6" Weight: 175 Origin: International Free Agent, 2013

YEAR	TEAM	LVL	AGE	W	L	SV	G	GS	IP	H	HR	BB/9	K/9	K	GB%	BABIP
2018	BNG	AA	23	0	3	0	7	7	38	31	3	2.4	9.9	42	41.0%	.289
2018	REA	AA	23	4	6	0	19	19	102	96	7	4.5	7.3	83	44.8%	.309
2020	NYM	MLB	25	0	1	1	4	0	11^1	14	5	7.1	10.3	13	34.3%	.310
2021 FS	NYM	MLB	26	2	3	0	57	0	50	48	8	5.2	8.4	46	40.0%	.290
2021 DC	NYM	MLB	26	1	1	0	34	0	29	28	5	5.2	8.4	27	40.0%	.290

Comparables: Bryan Mitchell, Adrian Houser, Myles Jaye

While there were signs Kilomé could eventually contribute at the major-league level, he gave up at least two runs in each of his four relief appearances during his post-TJS debut season. Suffice to say he's not guaranteed a big-league spot in 2021.

YEAR	TEAM	LVL	AGE	WHIP	ERA	DRA-	WARP	MPH	FB%	WHF	CSP
2018	BNG	AA	23	1.08	4.03	94	0.4				
2018	REA	AA	23	1.44	4.24	99	0.8				
2020	NYM	MLB	25	2.03	11.12	138	-0.1	96.4	53.7%	30.2%	
2021 FS	NYM	MLB	26	1.56	5.44	115	-0.2	96.4	53.7%	30.2%	44.6%
2021 DC	NYM	MLB	26	1.56	5.44	115	-0.1	96.4	53.7%	30.2%	44.6%

Franklyn Kilome, continued

Pitch Shape vs LHH

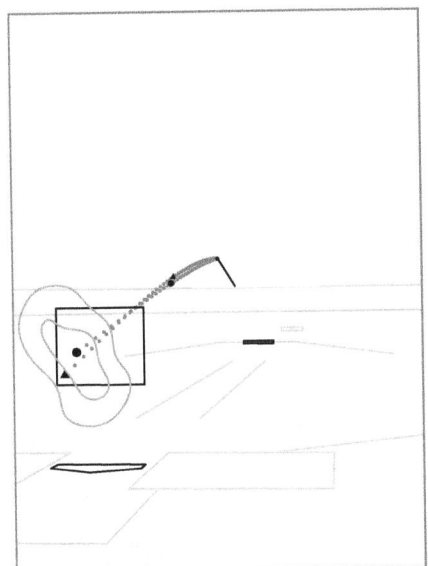

Pitch Shape vs RHH

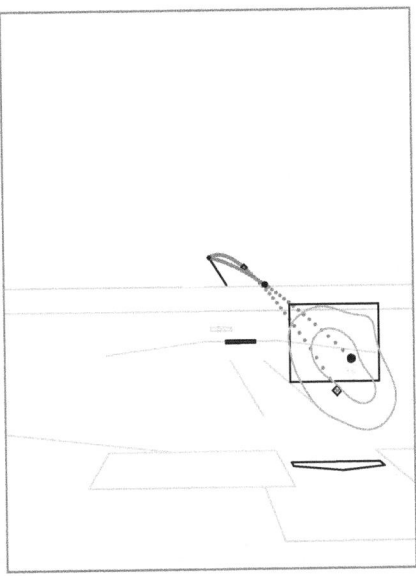

Type	Frequency	Velocity	H Movement	V Movement
● Fastball	53.7%	94.6 [106]	-7.7 [95]	-14 [103]
▲ Changeup	14.0%	85.4 [101]	-6.4 [128]	-28.2 [98]
▽ Slider	4.4%	86.9 [113]	-0.3 [79]	-26.8 [120]
◇ Curveball	27.9%	81.9 [113]	2.3 [79]	-45.7 [106]

New York Mets 2021

Aaron Loup LHP

Born: 12/19/87   Age: 33   Bats: L   Throws: L
Height: 5'11"   Weight: 210   Origin: Round 9, 2009 Draft (#280 overall)

YEAR	TEAM	LVL	AGE	W	L	SV	G	GS	IP	H	HR	BB/9	K/9	K	GB%	BABIP
2018	PHI	MLB	30	0	0	0	9	0	4	4	0	2.2	4.5	2	69.2%	.308
2018	TOR	MLB	30	0	0	0	50	0	35^2	44	4	3.3	10.6	42	48.1%	.385
2019	SD	MLB	31	0	0	0	4	0	3^1	2	0	2.7	13.5	5	57.1%	.286
2020	TB	MLB	32	3	2	0	24	0	25	17	3	1.4	7.9	22	39.4%	.230
2021 FS	NYM	MLB	33	2	2	0	57	0	50	46	6	3.0	9.2	50	47.3%	.298
2021 DC	NYM	MLB	33	2	2	0	47	0	40.7	37	4	3.0	9.2	41	47.3%	.298

Comparables: Ryan Tepera, Jeremy Jeffress, Anthony Bass

Loup wasn't projected to be anything more than organizational depth when he signed a minor-league deal with the Rays. Then a pandemic happened and half of the bullpen blew out their elbows. Loup ended up throwing more innings in the regular season for Tampa Bay than Diego Castillo, Jalen Beeks, Nick Anderson, Yonny Chirinos, Oliver Drake, Colin Poche, Chaz Roe and Jose Alvarado. Keeping it simple with a low-90s fastball or a cutter nine times out of 10, he worked efficiently and without much traffic. Most importantly, he showed an ability to hang in there against righties—that alone should be enough to net him a big-league deal by the time you pick up this book.

YEAR	TEAM	LVL	AGE	WHIP	ERA	DRA-	WARP	MPH	FB%	WHF	CSP
2018	PHI	MLB	30	1.25	4.50	155	-0.1	92.3	60.3%	15.2%	
2018	TOR	MLB	30	1.60	4.54	102	0.1	94.0	66.1%	27.4%	
2019	SD	MLB	31	0.90	0.00	90	0.0	93.2	43.4%	32.0%	
2020	TB	MLB	32	0.84	2.52	90	0.4	94.2	49.9%	19.8%	
2021 FS	NYM	MLB	33	1.26	3.83	88	0.6	94.0	55.5%	22.9%	52.4%
2021 DC	NYM	MLB	33	1.26	3.83	88	0.5	94.0	55.5%	22.9%	52.4%

Aaron Loup, continued

Pitch Shape vs LHH

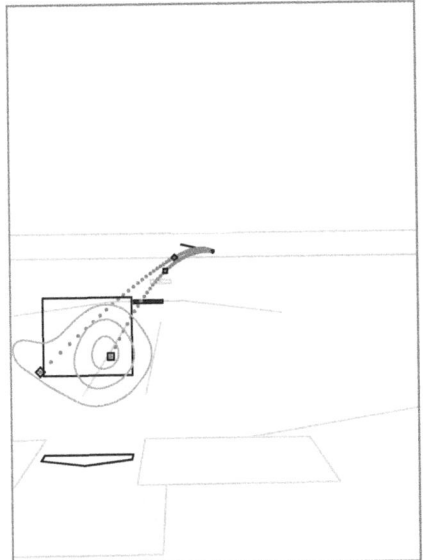

Pitch Shape vs RHH

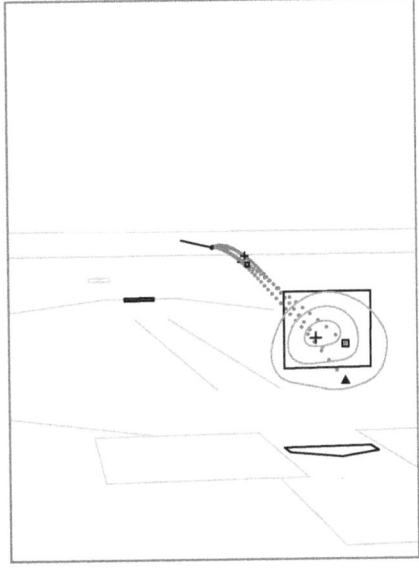

Type	Frequency	Velocity	H Movement	V Movement
☐ Sinker	49.9%	92.3 [99]	17.7 [66]	-25.9 [83]
+ Cutter	31.1%	85.6 [83]	0.1 [87]	-31.8 [70]
▲ Changeup	8.8%	80.9 [83]	16.7 [73]	-39.9 [66]
◇ Curveball	10.3%	77.8 [97]	-14.5 [128]	-42.1 [114]

Joey Lucchesi LHP

Born: 06/06/93 Age: 28 Bats: L Throws: L
Height: 6'5" Weight: 225 Origin: Round 4, 2016 Draft (#114 overall)

YEAR	TEAM	LVL	AGE	W	L	SV	G	GS	IP	H	HR	BB/9	K/9	K	GB%	BABIP
2018	LE	HI-A	25	0	0	0	1	1	4	0	0	0.0	13.5	6	66.7%	.000
2018	ELP	AAA	25	0	1	0	1	1	2²	7	1	13.5	6.8	2	27.3%	.600
2018	SD	MLB	25	8	9	0	26	26	130	125	23	3.0	10.0	145	44.7%	.310
2019	SD	MLB	26	10	10	0	30	30	163²	144	23	3.1	8.7	158	46.6%	.274
2020	SD	MLB	27	0	1	0	3	2	5²	13	0	3.2	7.9	5	37.5%	.542
2021 FS	NYM	MLB	28	9	8	0	26	26	150	140	22	3.4	9.1	151	45.3%	.294
2021 DC	NYM	MLB	28	4	4	0	9	16	72.7	68	10	3.4	9.1	73	45.3%	.294

Comparables: Andrew Suárez, Daniel Norris, Marco Gonzales

Lucchesi had an abysmal 2020. He appeared three times, allowed a run per inning and otherwise spent his summer at the alternate site—not what you would've expected from someone who made 56 starts the preceding two years. Lucchesi has shown enough promise in the past (he entered the year with a career 97 ERA+ and a 3.06 strikeout-to-walk ratio) to think he'll earn a rotation spot with some team, even if it seems increasingly likely that said team will reside somewhere other than San Diego.

YEAR	TEAM	LVL	AGE	WHIP	ERA	DRA-	WARP	MPH	FB%	WHF	CSP
2018	LE	HI-A	25	0.00	0.00	48	0.1				
2018	ELP	AAA	25	4.12	23.62	108	0.0				
2018	SD	MLB	25	1.29	4.08	84	2.3	92.3	64.2%	26.0%	
2019	SD	MLB	26	1.22	4.18	85	2.9	92.2	64.9%	25.6%	
2020	SD	MLB	27	2.65	7.94	100	0.0	91.4	65.0%	31.6%	
2021 FS	NYM	MLB	28	1.31	4.04	92	2.1	92.2	64.7%	26.0%	47.9%
2021 DC	NYM	MLB	28	1.31	4.04	92	1.0	92.2	64.7%	26.0%	47.9%

Joey Lucchesi, continued

Pitch Shape vs LHH

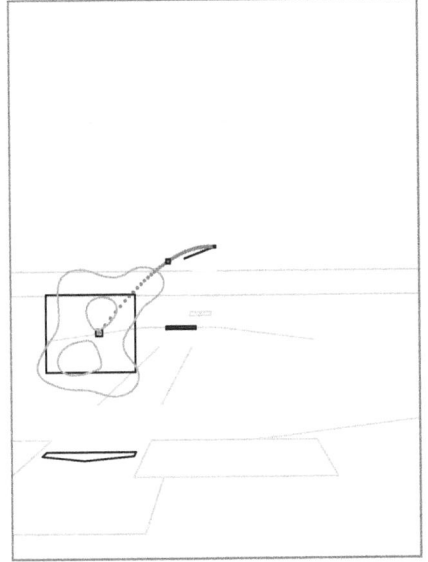

Pitch Shape vs RHH

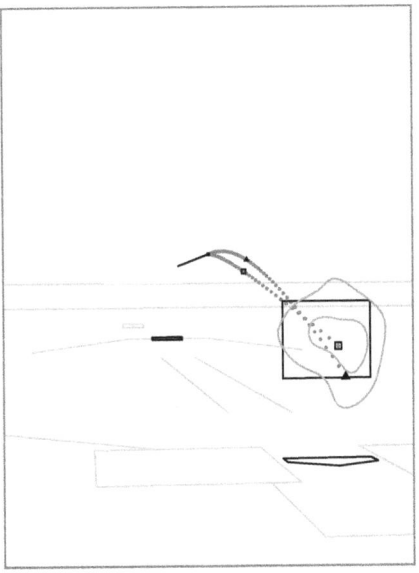

Type	Frequency	Velocity	H Movement	V Movement
● Fastball	8.9%	90.1 [92]	6.2 [103]	-18.6 [90]
□ Sinker	56.1%	89.9 [87]	12.2 [107]	-20.8 [99]
▲ Changeup	34.1%	77.6 [70]	-4.1 [184]	-41.9 [60]

Seth Lugo   RHP

Born: 11/17/89   Age: 31   Bats: R   Throws: R
Height: 6'4"   Weight: 225   Origin: Round 34, 2011 Draft (#1032 overall)

YEAR	TEAM	LVL	AGE	W	L	SV	G	GS	IP	H	HR	BB/9	K/9	K	GB%	BABIP
2018	NYM	MLB	28	3	4	3	54	5	101¹	81	9	2.5	9.1	103	45.8%	.270
2019	NYM	MLB	29	7	4	6	61	0	80	56	8	1.8	11.7	104	43.4%	.267
2020	NYM	MLB	30	3	4	3	16	7	36²	40	8	2.5	11.5	47	50.5%	.344
2021 FS	NYM	MLB	31	2	2	4	57	0	50	44	7	2.6	10.1	56	45.1%	.293
2021 DC	NYM	MLB	31	2	2	4	52	0	34.7	30	5	2.6	10.1	39	45.1%	.293

Comparables: Matt Andriese, Zack Godley, Erasmo Ramírez

Lugo may have established himself as a very effective reliever during 2019 and the start of 2020, but he's always stated a preference to return to the rotation. In August he got his wish, as Steven Matz was bumped and Lugo earned his chance to start again. The results were ... let's just say mixed, as he balanced five fair-to-good starts with two absolute disasters. His velocity only dipped a smidge in his move to the rotation, but he got battered during his second time through opposing lineups, struggling to limit his walks and looking less than comfortable while dealing with his midseason role change. It can be tough to balance Lugo's established dominance as a reliever against the potential for him to emerge as a mid-rotation starter, but either way he'd benefit greatly from having a defined role and sticking with it all season long, instead of being shifted after just a handful of appearances.

YEAR	TEAM	LVL	AGE	WHIP	ERA	DRA-	WARP	MPH	FB%	WHF	CSP
2018	NYM	MLB	28	1.08	2.66	85	1.4	96.5	48.6%	23.3%	
2019	NYM	MLB	29	0.90	2.70	55	2.3	96.7	56.7%	26.6%	
2020	NYM	MLB	30	1.36	5.15	76	0.8	96.2	55.4%	30.1%	
2021 FS	NYM	MLB	31	1.17	3.43	81	0.8	96.5	54.1%	26.8%	49.8%
2021 DC	NYM	MLB	31	1.17	3.43	81	0.6	96.5	54.1%	26.8%	49.8%

Seth Lugo, continued

Pitch Shape vs LHH

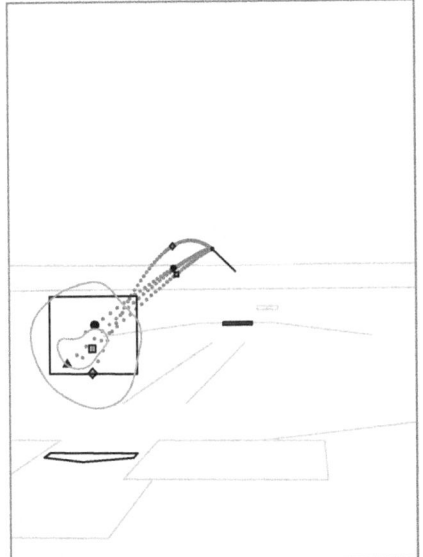

Pitch Shape vs RHH

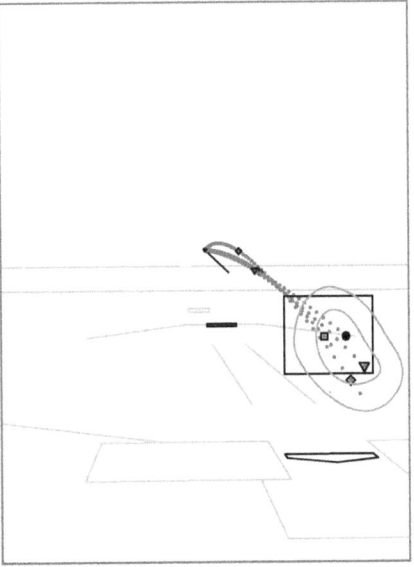

Type	Frequency	Velocity	H Movement	V Movement
● Fastball	33.6%	93.6 [103]	-7.3 [97]	-13.1 [106]
□ Sinker	21.8%	93.2 [104]	-14 [93]	-17.6 [109]
▲ Changeup	10.1%	87.4 [109]	-13.3 [92]	-24.7 [108]
▽ Slider	15.1%	87.8 [117]	2.7 [90]	-25.7 [123]
◇ Curveball	19.3%	78.6 [100]	11.2 [115]	-57.2 [80]

New York Mets 2021

Trevor May RHP
Born: 09/23/89 Age: 31 Bats: R Throws: R
Height: 6'5" Weight: 240 Origin: Round 4, 2008 Draft (#136 overall)

YEAR	TEAM	LVL	AGE	W	L	SV	G	GS	IP	H	HR	BB/9	K/9	K	GB%	BABIP
2018	ROC	AAA	28	0	4	2	13	4	27	24	2	5.3	8.3	25	39.0%	.293
2018	MIN	MLB	28	4	1	3	24	1	25^1	21	4	1.8	12.8	36	37.7%	.309
2019	MIN	MLB	29	5	3	2	65	0	64^1	43	8	3.6	11.1	79	34.2%	.233
2020	MIN	MLB	30	1	0	2	24	0	23^1	20	5	2.7	14.7	38	25.5%	.326
2021 FS	NYM	MLB	31	2	2	4	57	0	50	41	7	3.2	11.5	63	33.7%	.288
2021 DC	NYM	MLB	31	2	2	4	51	0	52.3	42	8	3.2	11.5	66	33.7%	.288

Comparables: Erasmo Ramírez, Matt Andriese, Alex Colomé

May's a valedictorian, electronic music artist, relief pitcher, occasional writer at MLB Trade Rumors and Twitch streamer—and judging by his Twitter metrics, it's the last of those he's most famous for. On the field, @IamTrevorMay is your prototypical modern-day reliever: He strikes out a lotta dudes but gives up too many homers to be more than a solid option in middle relief. If there's a path forward, it might be by becoming a bit more of a throwback. Like just about everyone, he increased the usage of his slider at the expense of his fastball last season. Unlike everyone, it's unclear that this tradeoff benefits DJ HEYBEEF. He's steadily added velocity to his heater in recent years, and now sits comfortably in the mid-90s. Moreover, he's adept at locating his high-spinner up in the zone, where he notched a very high 22 percent whiff rate last year—better than any of his offspeed pitches. Perhaps he can share his thoughts on that over a game of Call of Duty?

YEAR	TEAM	LVL	AGE	WHIP	ERA	DRA-	WARP	MPH	FB%	WHF	CSP
2018	ROC	AAA	28	1.48	4.00	76	0.5				
2018	MIN	MLB	28	1.03	3.20	66	0.6	95.5	59.2%	32.7%	
2019	MIN	MLB	29	1.07	2.94	81	1.0	97.5	62.9%	30.1%	
2020	MIN	MLB	30	1.16	3.86	85	0.4	97.9	51.7%	43.0%	
2021 FS	NYM	MLB	31	1.18	3.46	81	0.8	97.4	59.0%	34.3%	45.9%
2021 DC	NYM	MLB	31	1.18	3.46	81	0.8	97.4	59.0%	34.3%	45.9%

Trevor May, continued

Pitch Shape vs LHH

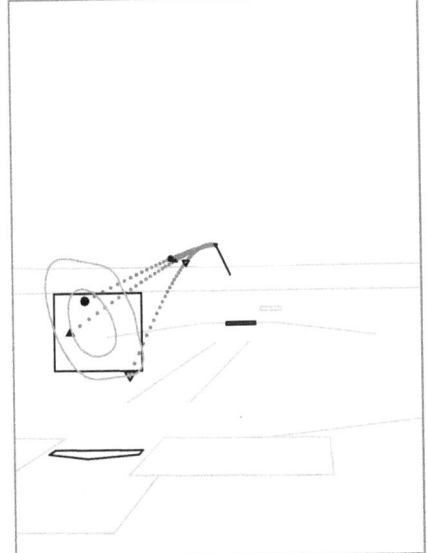

Pitch Shape vs RHH

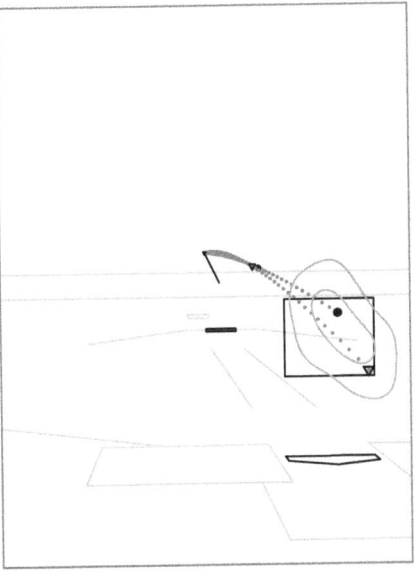

Type	Frequency	Velocity	H Movement	V Movement
● Fastball	51.7%	96.5 [113]	-6.6 [101]	-11.5 [110]
▲ Changeup	15.6%	87.9 [111]	-9.5 [112]	-19 [123]
▽ Slider	32.7%	85.4 [107]	4.3 [96]	-36.2 [93]

Corey Oswalt   RHP

Born: 09/03/93   Age: 27   Bats: R   Throws: R
Height: 6'5"   Weight: 250   Origin: Round 7, 2012 Draft (#230 overall)

YEAR	TEAM	LVL	AGE	W	L	SV	G	GS	IP	H	HR	BB/9	K/9	K	GB%	BABIP
2018	LV	AAA	24	4	4	0	11	11	52^1	58	9	3.4	8.9	52	43.9%	.331
2018	NYM	MLB	24	3	3	0	17	12	64^2	69	14	2.8	6.3	45	40.8%	.278
2019	BRK	SS	25	0	0	0	2	2	6	6	0	4.5	10.5	7	27.8%	.333
2019	SYR	AAA	25	10	4	0	16	16	86^2	84	9	1.6	8.2	79	43.8%	.305
2019	NYM	MLB	25	0	1	0	2	0	6^2	9	1	8.1	6.8	5	34.8%	.364
2020	NYM	MLB	26	0	0	0	4	1	13	14	3	1.4	7.6	11	36.6%	.289
2021 FS	NYM	MLB	27	2	2	0	57	0	50	49	8	2.7	7.9	43	40.8%	.287
2021 DC	NYM	MLB	27	1	1	0	27	0	11.3	11	2	2.7	7.9	10	40.8%	.287

Comparables: Luis Perdomo, Chase De Jong, Luis Cessa

The New York Mets' injury-prone starting rotation has often led the team to look for a proverbial "break-glass-in-case-of-emergency" fire extinguisher in human form. Enter Oswalt, ideally that man-shaped fire extinguisher, but instead of being full of suppressant, he's filled to the brim with hanging sliders, the pitching equivalent of butane.

YEAR	TEAM	LVL	AGE	WHIP	ERA	DRA-	WARP	MPH	FB%	WHF	CSP
2018	LV	AAA	24	1.49	6.02	136	-0.5				
2018	NYM	MLB	24	1.38	5.85	128	-0.4	92.5	67.0%	16.6%	
2019	BRK	SS	25	1.50	1.50	107	0.0				
2019	SYR	AAA	25	1.14	2.91	65	3.0				
2019	NYM	MLB	25	2.25	12.15	115	0.0	93.8	65.7%	15.8%	
2020	NYM	MLB	26	1.23	4.85	114	0.0	93.8	53.4%	29.7%	
2021 FS	NYM	MLB	27	1.29	4.34	99	0.3	93.2	62.2%	20.9%	44.7%
2021 DC	NYM	MLB	27	1.29	4.34	99	0.1	93.2	62.2%	20.9%	44.7%

Corey Oswalt, continued

Pitch Shape vs LHH

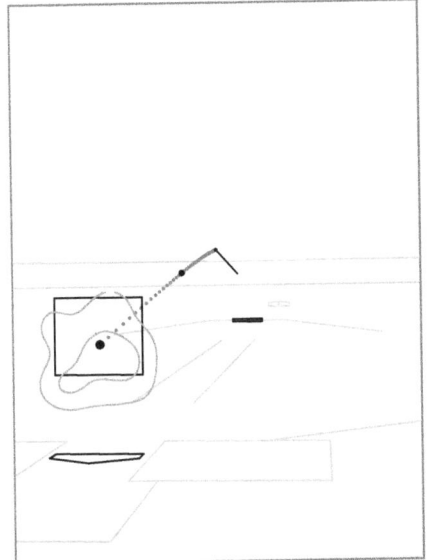

Pitch Shape vs RHH

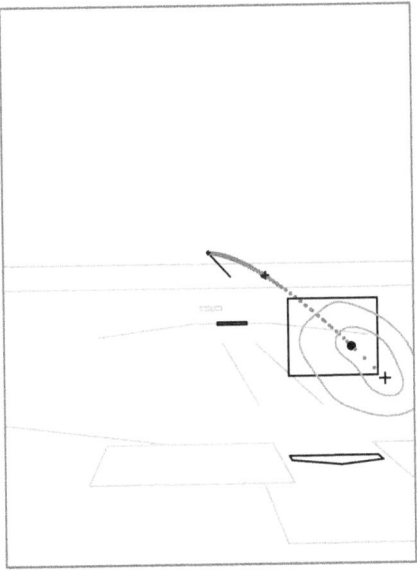

Type	Frequency	Velocity	H Movement	V Movement
● Fastball	47.5%	92.4 [99]	-9.9 [85]	-14.9 [101]
□ Sinker	5.8%	92.1 [99]	-13.3 [98]	-18.8 [106]
+ Cutter	28.3%	88 [98]	-2 [75]	-26.9 [89]
▲ Changeup	16.6%	85.7 [102]	-10.7 [106]	-31.2 [90]

David Peterson LHP

Born: 09/03/95   Age: 25   Bats: L   Throws: L
Height: 6'6"   Weight: 240   Origin: Round 1, 2017 Draft (#20 overall)

YEAR	TEAM	LVL	AGE	W	L	SV	G	GS	IP	H	HR	BB/9	K/9	K	GB%	BABIP
2018	COL	LO-A	22	1	4	0	9	9	59^1	46	1	1.7	8.6	57	65.0%	.285
2018	STL	HI-A	22	6	6	0	13	13	68^2	74	1	2.5	7.6	58	60.3%	.340
2019	BNG	AA	23	3	6	0	24	24	116	119	9	2.9	9.5	122	52.0%	.342
2020	NYM	MLB	24	6	2	0	10	9	49^2	36	5	4.3	7.2	40	44.2%	.233
2021 FS	NYM	MLB	25	9	8	0	26	26	150	141	21	4.5	8.1	135	46.6%	.286
2021 DC	NYM	MLB	25	6	6	0	12	21	109.3	103	15	4.5	8.1	98	46.6%	.286

Comparables: Nick Margevicius, Josh Fleming, Eric Lauer

Jumping from Double-A to the majors isn't the great leap that it used to be, but it's still quite the gap to cover, even if you're a high-floor left-handed starting pitcher with a deep enough arsenal to make it through the order a couple of times. But Peterson's wiles and his slider proved enough to get by at the back of the Mets' rotation, even if he couldn't approximate his minor-league ground ball or strikeout rates in his first go-round in the majors. The two strong starts to close out the year and the sharp ERA are tantalizing, but the lack of dominant stuff means that his ceiling probably isn't much higher than that of a fourth starter.

YEAR	TEAM	LVL	AGE	WHIP	ERA	DRA-	WARP	MPH	FB%	WHF	CSP
2018	COL	LO-A	22	0.96	1.82	72	1.2				
2018	STL	HI-A	22	1.35	4.33	83	1.0				
2019	BNG	AA	23	1.34	4.19	116	-1.0				
2020	NYM	MLB	24	1.21	3.44	110	0.2	94.2	53.2%	26.2%	
2021 FS	NYM	MLB	25	1.45	4.68	103	1.2	94.2	53.2%	26.2%	44.8%
2021 DC	NYM	MLB	25	1.45	4.68	103	0.8	94.2	53.2%	26.2%	44.8%

David Peterson, continued

Pitch Shape vs LHH

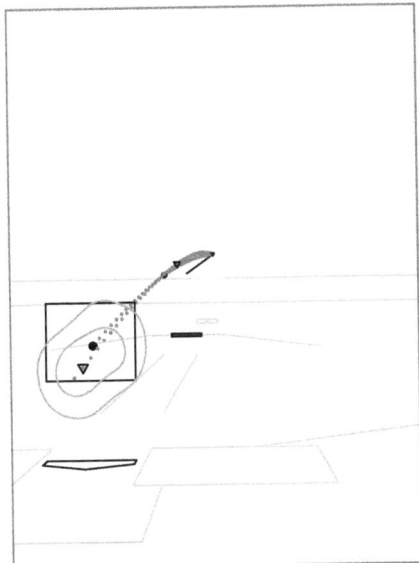

Pitch Shape vs RHH

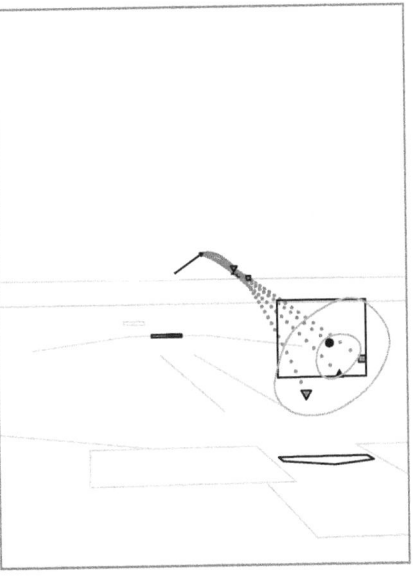

Type	Frequency	Velocity	H Movement	V Movement
● Fastball	34.0%	92.3 [99]	10 [84]	-16.3 [97]
☐ Sinker	19.2%	92 [98]	14.2 [92]	-19.4 [104]
▲ Changeup	18.7%	83.8 [95]	14.7 [84]	-28.1 [98]
▽ Slider	25.9%	81.4 [89]	-5.9 [103]	-38.9 [85]

Rick Porcello   RHP
Born: 12/27/88   Age: 32   Bats: R   Throws: R
Height: 6'5"   Weight: 205   Origin: Round 1, 2007 Draft (#27 overall)

YEAR	TEAM	LVL	AGE	W	L	SV	G	GS	IP	H	HR	BB/9	K/9	K	GB%	BABIP
2018	BOS	MLB	29	17	7	0	33	33	191^1	177	27	2.3	8.9	190	44.0%	.286
2019	BOS	MLB	30	14	12	0	32	32	174^1	198	31	2.3	7.4	143	38.0%	.310
2020	NYM	MLB	31	1	7	0	12	12	59	74	5	2.3	8.2	54	40.5%	.373
2021 FS	NYM	MLB	32	9	8	0	26	26	150	152	26	2.2	7.8	130	40.0%	.293
2021 DC	NYM	MLB	32	9	8	0	28	28	140	142	24	2.2	7.8	121	40.0%	.293

Comparables: Frank Viola, Brad Radke, Scott Baker

Given the Mets' injury issues and Porcello's New Jersey roots, it seemed like only a matter of time before the veteran right-hander found his way to his hometown team. But Porcello was paid more like a mid-rotation starter than the back-of-the-rotation profile he's shown since his Cy Young win in Boston. He leaned harder on his slider than usual, and there was some weirdness in his batted ball profile: He was top-five in the majors in both line drive percentage (bad!) and infield fly percentage (good!), but was worst in the National League at stranding a runner once they reached base. Overall, it was a bust of a year for the local kid, and his next free agent contract is much more likely to reflect his diminished standing than his previous one.

YEAR	TEAM	LVL	AGE	WHIP	ERA	DRA-	WARP	MPH	FB%	WHF	CSP
2018	BOS	MLB	29	1.18	4.28	89	2.8	92.8	50.0%	20.4%	
2019	BOS	MLB	30	1.39	5.52	124	-0.5	92.5	56.5%	18.0%	
2020	NYM	MLB	31	1.51	5.64	83	1.1	92.6	53.2%	15.5%	
2021 FS	NYM	MLB	32	1.26	4.22	98	1.6	92.6	54.0%	18.0%	49.1%
2021 DC	NYM	MLB	32	1.26	4.22	98	1.5	92.6	54.0%	18.0%	49.1%

Rick Porcello, continued

Pitch Shape vs LHH

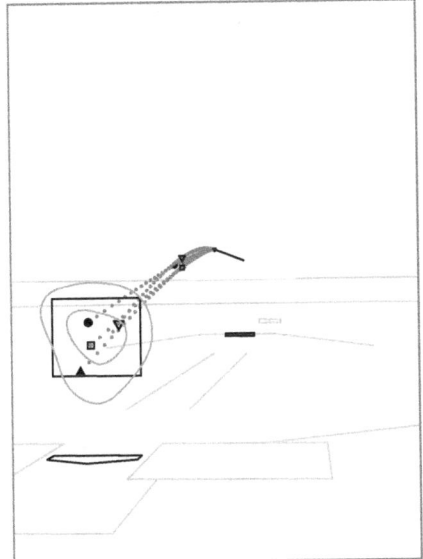

Pitch Shape vs RHH

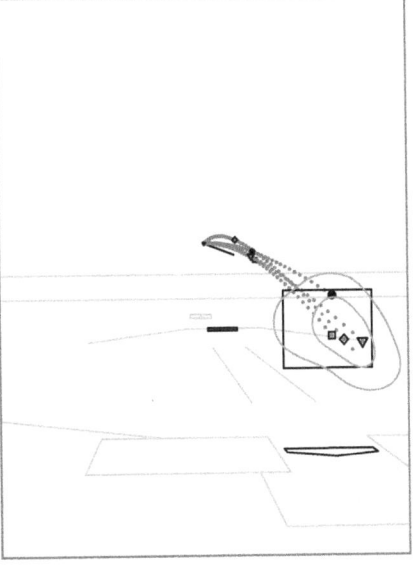

Type	Frequency	Velocity	H Movement	V Movement
● Fastball	10.8%	91.7 [97]	-7 [98]	-14.7 [101]
□ Sinker	42.3%	90.2 [89]	-14 [93]	-21.2 [98]
▲ Changeup	12.5%	81.9 [87]	-13 [93]	-30.4 [92]
▽ Slider	29.2%	86.4 [111]	2.5 [89]	-26 [122]
◇ Curveball	5.1%	75.1 [86]	9.1 [106]	-48.4 [100]

Sean Reid-Foley   RHP

Born: 08/30/95   Age: 25   Bats: R   Throws: R
Height: 6'3"   Weight: 230   Origin: Round 2, 2014 Draft (#49 overall)

YEAR	TEAM	LVL	AGE	W	L	SV	G	GS	IP	H	HR	BB/9	K/9	K	GB%	BABIP
2018	NH	AA	22	5	0	0	8	8	44.1	27	3	4.1	10.6	52	51.5%	.240
2018	BUF	AAA	22	7	5	0	16	16	85.1	76	5	3.2	10.3	98	43.0%	.318
2018	TOR	MLB	22	2	4	0	7	7	33.1	31	6	5.7	11.3	42	36.0%	.312
2019	BUF	AAA	23	3	5	0	20	19	89	78	13	6.6	10.6	105	43.0%	.294
2019	TOR	MLB	23	2	4	0	9	6	31.2	33	5	6.0	8.0	28	42.4%	.298
2020	TOR	MLB	24	1	0	0	5	0	6.2	3	0	8.1	8.1	6	61.1%	.167
2021 FS	NYM	MLB	25	2	3	0	57	0	50	45	7	5.5	9.3	51	42.5%	.289
2021 DC	NYM	MLB	25	1	1	0	22	0	29	26	4	5.5	9.3	30	42.5%	.289

Comparables: Touki Toussaint, Jake Thompson, Tyler Mahle

Reid-Foley found himself squeezed out of a suddenly overstocked post-deadline Toronto bullpen, and it was probably for the best for all parties, given the reliever's peripherals and past experience. Despite the limited showing, there was reason for encouragement: He simplified his pitch mix, abandoning a feckless curveball and leaning more on the beginning reliever's toolkit, fastball and slider. He also enjoyed the velocity increase that bullpen work sometimes provides, providing a clear path for his future with the organization. The catch? Reid-Foley had a hard enough time throwing straight before he threw harder.

YEAR	TEAM	LVL	AGE	WHIP	ERA	DRA-	WARP	MPH	FB%	WHF	CSP
2018	NH	AA	22	1.06	2.03	77	0.9				
2018	BUF	AAA	22	1.24	3.90	70	2.0				
2018	TOR	MLB	22	1.56	5.13	110	0.1	95.8	63.2%	29.1%	
2019	BUF	AAA	23	1.61	6.47	101	1.5				
2019	TOR	MLB	23	1.71	4.26	155	-0.6	94.8	50.2%	23.9%	
2020	TOR	MLB	24	1.35	1.35	89	0.1	96.1	61.7%	30.0%	
2021 FS	NYM	MLB	25	1.53	5.07	109	0.0	95.3	55.9%	26.5%	44.4%
2021 DC	NYM	MLB	25	1.53	5.07	109	0.1	95.3	55.9%	26.5%	44.4%

Sean Reid-Foley, continued

Pitch Shape vs LHH

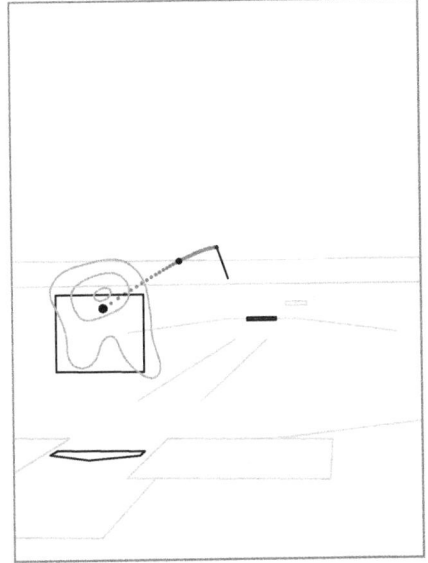

Pitch Shape vs RHH

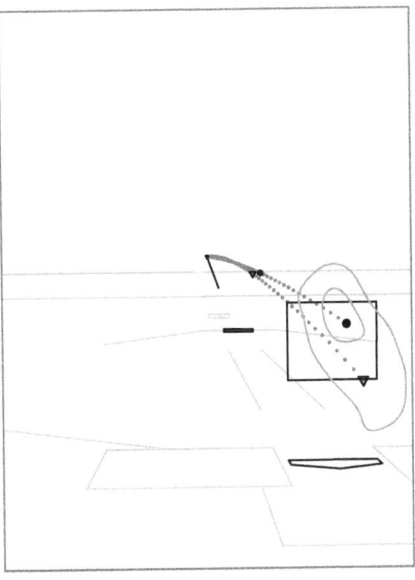

Type	Frequency	Velocity	H Movement	V Movement
● Fastball	59.9%	94.4 [106]	-5.2 [107]	-12.3 [108]
▲ Changeup	5.8%	86.3 [105]	-12.2 [98]	-25.2 [106]
▽ Slider	31.4%	86 [109]	3.5 [93]	-32.4 [104]

Justin Wilson LHP

Born: 08/18/87   Age: 33   Bats: L   Throws: L
Height: 6'2"   Weight: 205   Origin: Round 5, 2008 Draft (#144 overall)

YEAR	TEAM	LVL	AGE	W	L	SV	G	GS	IP	H	HR	BB/9	K/9	K	GB%	BABIP
2018	CHC	MLB	30	4	5	0	71	0	54²	45	5	5.4	11.4	69	35.8%	.310
2019	NYM	MLB	31	4	2	4	45	0	39	33	4	4.4	10.2	44	50.5%	.299
2020	NYM	MLB	32	2	1	0	23	0	19²	18	1	4.1	10.5	23	43.4%	.333
2021 FS	NYM	MLB	33	2	2	0	57	0	50	42	5	4.4	10.5	58	44.0%	.294
2021 DC	NYM	MLB	33	2	2	0	57	0	49.7	42	5	4.4	10.5	58	44.0%	.294

Comparables: Jeremy Jeffress, Bryan Shaw, Anthony Bass

A bastion of consistency in a New York bullpen that was anything but, Wilson put up another solid season, putting aside both the notions that his 2018 run with the Cubs was anything but a fluke, or that he'll ever return to the role of top-flight closer rather than a well-rounded fireman. He's settled as a southpaw without big splits and enough minor injury flags to warrant judicious use, but remains more effective and reliable than many of the boom-or-bust relief options floating about the majority of the majors.

YEAR	TEAM	LVL	AGE	WHIP	ERA	DRA-	WARP	MPH	FB%	WHF	CSP
2018	CHC	MLB	30	1.43	3.46	103	0.2	96.1	75.4%	26.8%	
2019	NYM	MLB	31	1.33	2.54	71	0.8	96.6	52.4%	25.6%	
2020	NYM	MLB	32	1.37	3.66	79	0.4	96.6	59.4%	24.7%	
2021 FS	NYM	MLB	33	1.34	3.67	86	0.6	96.4	61.4%	25.7%	50.5%
2021 DC	NYM	MLB	33	1.34	3.67	86	0.6	96.4	61.4%	25.7%	50.5%

Justin Wilson, continued

Pitch Shape vs LHH

Pitch Shape vs RHH

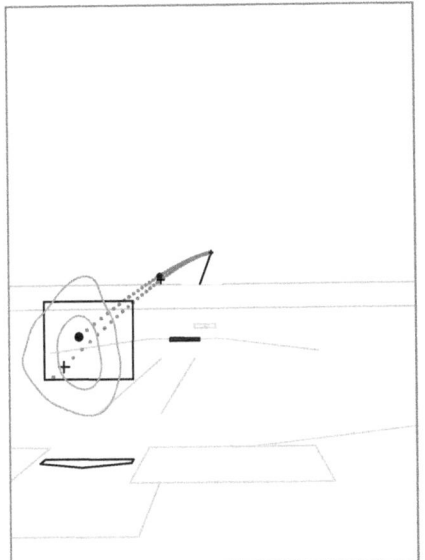
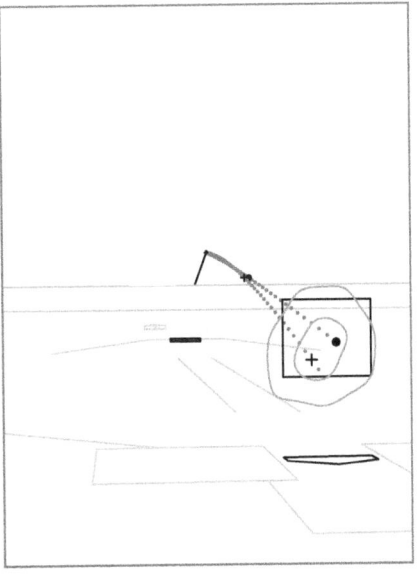

Type	Frequency	Velocity	H Movement	V Movement
● Fastball	58.7%	95.1 [108]	5.7 [105]	-10.5 [113]
+ Cutter	36.7%	90.9 [116]	-2.6 [105]	-19.6 [118]

Jordan Yamamoto RHP

Born: 05/11/96 Age: 25 Bats: R Throws: R
Height: 6'0" Weight: 185 Origin: Round 12, 2014 Draft (#356 overall)

YEAR	TEAM	LVL	AGE	W	L	SV	G	GS	IP	H	HR	BB/9	K/9	K	GB%	BABIP
2018	MRL	ROK	22	1	0	0	3	3	11	5	1	1.6	12.3	15	59.1%	.190
2018	JUP	HI-A	22	4	1	0	7	7	40^2	26	0	1.8	10.4	47	41.2%	.271
2018	JAX	AA	22	1	0	0	3	3	17	12	1	2.1	12.2	23	45.0%	.282
2019	JAX	AA	23	3	5	0	12	12	65^1	53	7	3.4	8.8	64	46.0%	.275
2019	MIA	MLB	23	4	5	0	15	15	78^2	54	11	4.1	9.4	82	36.6%	.225
2020	MIA	MLB	24	0	1	0	4	3	11^1	27	8	5.6	10.3	13	31.9%	.487
2021 FS	NYM	MLB	25	2	3	0	57	0	50	47	8	4.6	9.0	50	37.5%	.288
2021 DC	NYM	MLB	25	2	2	0	40	3	13.3	12	2	4.6	9.0	13	37.5%	.288

Comparables: Mitch Keller, Albert Abreu, Robert Dugger

There were hidden costs to the way the 2020 season unfolded. Yamamoto seemed to be emerging as a viable mid-rotation option in 2019 and everything looked fine in spring. By the time summer camp rolled around, he just wasn't the same pitcher. His grip on a rotation spot quickly slipped away and he ended up at the alternate site to rebuild arm strength. When called upon later in the season, it became clear why the Marlins had lost confidence in him. His velocity was consistently down a couple ticks and he got various levels of lit up in every game he pitched in, culminating in a 13-run relief bombing. He'll be hoping a more normal offseason can get things back on track.

YEAR	TEAM	LVL	AGE	WHIP	ERA	DRA-	WARP	MPH	FB%	WHF	CSP
2018	MRL	ROK	22	0.64	2.45						
2018	JUP	HI-A	22	0.84	1.55	60	1.1				
2018	JAX	AA	22	0.94	2.12	84	0.3				
2019	JAX	AA	23	1.19	3.58	93	0.3				
2019	MIA	MLB	23	1.14	4.46	72	1.9	93.6	67.9%	22.7%	
2020	MIA	MLB	24	3.00	18.26	182	-0.4	92.2	61.1%	19.8%	
2021 FS	NYM	MLB	25	1.45	4.91	107	0.0	93.2	66.3%	22.1%	46.8%
2021 DC	NYM	MLB	25	1.45	4.91	107	0.1	93.2	66.3%	22.1%	46.8%

Jordan Yamamoto, continued

Pitch Shape vs LHH

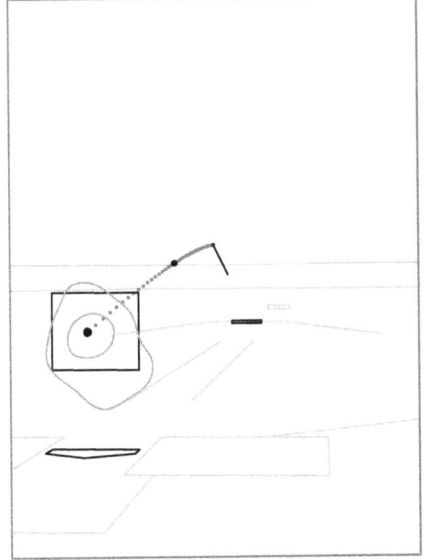

Pitch Shape vs RHH

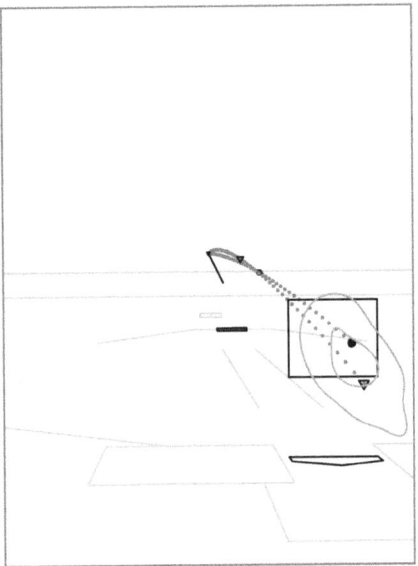

Type	Frequency	Velocity	H Movement	V Movement
● Fastball	38.9%	90.1 [92]	-5.4 [106]	-16.5 [96]
+ Cutter	20.4%	86.2 [86]	2.2 [102]	-29.5 [79]
▽ Slider	21.5%	78.1 [74]	15.5 [139]	-46.4 [63]
◇ Curveball	15.2%	74.3 [83]	11.1 [114]	-58.5 [78]

PLAYER COMMENTS WITHOUT GRAPHS

Albert Almora Jr. CF
Born: 04/16/94 Age: 27 Bats: R Throws: R
Height: 6'2" Weight: 190 Origin: Round 1, 2012 Draft (#6 overall)

YEAR	TEAM	LVL	AGE	PA	R	2B	3B	HR	RBI	BB	K	SB	CS	AVG/OBP/SLG
2018	CHC	MLB	24	479	62	24	1	5	41	24	83	1	3	.286/.323/.378
2019	IOW	AAA	25	54	6	3	1	0	2	4	7	2	1	.224/.283/.327
2019	CHC	MLB	25	363	41	11	1	12	32	16	62	2	1	.236/.271/.381
2020	CHC	MLB	26	34	4	1	0	0	1	3	9	0	0	.167/.265/.200
2021 FS	NYM	MLB	27	600	73	27	2	16	72	34	117	2	2	.252/.300/.395
2021 DC	NYM	MLB	27	158	19	7	0	4	19	9	30	0	1	.252/.300/.395

Comparables: Randy Kutcher, Hiram Bocachica, Ken Gerhart

Once upon a time, way back in 2013, the top of the Cubs' farm system rankings looked like this: 1. Albert Almora, 2. Javier Báez, 3. Jorge Soler. The rest of the list isn't all that important (OK, Dan Vogelbach was fifth), but the next year Almora ranked third behind just Baez and Kris Bryant. He was a top-50 prospect his first three years in organized ball and a top-101 guy five times. This is all to say that Almora once held a lot of promise. Prospects will break your heart, as we all know, and after more than 1,300 career plate appearances we have ample evidence that Almora is a replacement-level outfielder. The contending Cubs finally saw enough in 2020, and he was demoted at the end of August after the acquisition of Cameron Maybin. Almora's glove still provides value, and he's likely to continue to carve out opportunities as a fourth outfielder-type, but the days of waiting on him to live up to his lofty potential are long gone.

YEAR	TEAM	LVL	AGE	PA	DRC+	BABIP	BRR	FRAA	WARP
2018	CHC	MLB	24	479	84	.337	-0.1	CF(137): 2.5, LF(2): -0.1	1.0
2019	IOW	AAA	25	54	56	.262	0.0	CF(12): 2.0	0.1
2019	CHC	MLB	25	363	72	.255	-0.4	CF(125): 2.0	0.2
2020	CHC	MLB	26	34	72	.238	0.0	CF(28): 1.2	0.0
2021 FS	NYM	MLB	27	600	88	.293	-0.6	CF 2, LF 0	1.2
2021 DC	NYM	MLB	27	158	88	.293	-0.1	CF 1	0.3

Aaron Altherr CF

Born: 01/14/91   Age: 30   Bats: R   Throws: R
Height: 6'5"   Weight: 215   Origin: Round 9, 2009 Draft (#287 overall)

YEAR	TEAM	LVL	AGE	PA	R	2B	3B	HR	RBI	BB	K	SB	CS	AVG/OBP/SLG
2018	LHV	AAA	27	134	15	5	0	2	12	14	37	4	0	.244/.321/.336
2018	PHI	MLB	27	285	28	11	1	8	38	36	91	3	2	.181/.295/.333
2019	SYR	AAA	28	88	9	5	1	4	13	10	16	3	2	.270/.375/.527
2019	PHI	MLB	28	30	2	1	0	0	1	1	9	0	0	.034/.067/.069
2019	NYM	MLB	28	35	6	1	0	1	2	2	15	0	0	.129/.200/.258
2019	SF	MLB	28	1	0	0	0	0	0	0	1	0	0	.000/.000/.000
2020	NC	KBO	29	546	90	20	7	31	108	44	149	22	3	.278/.352/.541
2021 FS	NYM	MLB	30	600	64	22	2	19	67	60	183	9	4	.210/.305/.371

Comparables: Jayson Werth, Byron Browne, Kevin Roberson

In the majors, Altherr's trouble with the slow stuff ran him out of the league, which made him a bit of an odd choice for a KBO signee. There's not much velo in the Korean game, but every hurler has a steady supply of junk, and after a terrible first couple of weeks, the Dinos had to have been at least a little worried about their import center fielder. Fortunately for all parties, he soon found his footing. While he nearly led the league in strikeout percentage, he also hit 30 bombs and played the circuit's best center field. Somewhat bizarrely, the early-season slump stuck him in the eight-hole for most of the season even as he grew into one of the team's toughest outs. His three-run shot in Game 1 of the Korean series was a vital part of the Dinos title run, and provided that a late-season mask controversy—he refused to wear it during a post-game press conference—is all water under the bridge, a return to Changwon seems to make sense for all parties.

YEAR	TEAM	LVL	AGE	PA	DRC+	BABIP	BRR	FRAA	WARP
2018	LHV	AAA	27	134	90	.333	-0.6	CF(21): -0.6, LF(8): 2.7, RF(2): -0.2	0.2
2018	PHI	MLB	27	285	73	.247	-1.2	RF(68): -4.2, CF(11): -0.4, LF(6): 0.4	-0.8
2019	SYR	AAA	28	88	114	.291	-0.8	CF(11): -0.7, RF(11): 2.1, LF(3): 0.9	0.5
2019	PHI	MLB	28	30	58	.050	0.0	CF(8): -0.3, RF(4): 0.2, LF(1): -0.0	-0.1
2019	NYM	MLB	28	35	42	.188	0.0	LF(13): -0.5, CF(8): -0.1, RF(2): -0.2	-0.2
2019	SF	MLB	28	1	28				0.0
2020	NC	KBO	29	546					
2021 FS	NYM	MLB	30	600	86	.281	0.2	RF 1, CF 0	0.6

Francisco Alvarez   C

Born: 11/19/01   Age: 19   Bats: R   Throws: R
Height: 5'11"   Weight: 220   Origin: International Free Agent, 2018

YEAR	TEAM	LVL	AGE	PA	R	2B	3B	HR	RBI	BB	K	SB	CS	AVG/OBP/SLG
2019	MTS	ROK	17	31	8	4	0	2	10	4	4	0	1	.462/.548/.846
2019	KNG	ROK+	17	151	24	6	0	5	16	17	33	1	1	.289/.385/.453
2021 FS	NYM	MLB	19	600	47	19	2	9	50	36	194	1	2	.196/.251/.290

Comparables: Wil Myers, Joey Gallo, Oscar Hernández

The missed development time for Alvarez, already considered an "advanced" catching prospect in most circles, might be less of a factor than for most backstop prospects. While losing a full season of pro ball and the opportunity to build on his outstanding performance as a 17-year-old, Alvarez still has all the tools (and time) to develop into an offense-first backstop with the athleticism and frame to stick behind the plate. He signed with the Sydney Blue Sox to get some reps over the winter but never made it on the field, so the few weeks he had at the Mets' alternate site and fall instructs were the only chance he had in the back half of 2020 to build on the electric start to his pro career.

YEAR	TEAM	LVL	AGE	PA	DRC+	BABIP	BRR	FRAA	WARP
2019	MTS	ROK	17	31		.500			
2019	KNG	ROK+	17	151		.356			
2021 FS	NYM	MLB	19	600	49	.280	-0.5	C 1	-1.4

Norichika Aoki 青木 宣親   RF

Born: 01/05/82   Age: 39   Bats: L   Throws: R
Height: 5'9"   Weight: 180   Origin:

YEAR	TEAM	LVL	AGE	PA	R	2B	3B	HR	RBI	BB	K	SB	CS	AVG/OBP/SLG
2018	YKL	NPB	36	567	85	37	3	10	67	51	48	3	4	.327/.409/.475
2019	YKL	NPB	37	565	84	19	2	16	58	61	72	1	2	.297/.385/.442
2020	YKL	NPB	38	425	64	30	1	18	51	62	51	2	1	.317/.424/.557
2021							No projection							

If Aoki were a fictional player in a baseball manga, 2020 would be the grand finale; a veteran, after a lengthy tenure in the big leagues, returning to his struggling first professional team and putting up some of the best offensive numbers in the league, including career-highs in OPS and ISO at the age of 38. Well, aside from the part where instead of winning the pennant on the final day, the Swallows finish 25 games back. While the inevitable decline awaits on the horizon, Aoki, who was been an above-average-to-plus regular in each of the last three seasons upon his return to Yakult, seems to have some gas left in the tank and should bridge the gap between now and the next great Swallows team.

YEAR	TEAM	LVL	AGE	PA	DRC+	BABIP	BRR	FRAA	WARP
2018	YKL	NPB	36	567					
2019	YKL	NPB	37	565					
2020	YKL	NPB	38	425					
2021					*No projection*				

Brett Baty 3B

Born: 11/13/99 Age: 21 Bats: L Throws: R
Height: 6'3" Weight: 210 Origin: Round 1, 2019 Draft (#12 overall)

YEAR	TEAM	LVL	AGE	PA	R	2B	3B	HR	RBI	BB	K	SB	CS	AVG/OBP/SLG
2019	MTS	ROK	19	25	5	3	0	1	8	5	6	0	0	.350/.480/.650
2019	KNG	ROK+	19	186	30	12	2	6	22	24	56	0	0	.226/.344/.445
2019	BRK	SS	19	17	2	1	0	0	3	6	3	0	0	.200/.529/.300
2021 FS	*NYM*	*MLB*	*21*	*600*	*45*	*20*	*2*	*7*	*45*	*52*	*231*	*0*	*1*	*.168/.249/.259*

Comparables: Joey Gallo, Jamie Romak, Joc Pederson

Baty's lost season at least ended on a high note: he was added to the Mets' player pool in late August, just in time to get a few reps with the pro staff before the season came to a close. He'll never be Brett *Glovey*, so the big Texan has to develop his hit tool to support his big-time raw power; despite admiring Adrian Beltre as a youngster, the chances of becoming a gloveman like his Hall-of-Fame-bound hero are markedly low. Already entering his age-21 season and with only 211 plate appearances beyond high school, Baty remains a high-variance prospect who needs far more time facing professional breaking pitches than just the handful he experienced this past September.

YEAR	TEAM	LVL	AGE	PA	DRC+	BABIP	BRR	FRAA	WARP
2019	MTS	ROK	19	25		.462			
2019	KNG	ROK+	19	186		.312			
2019	BRK	SS	19	17	173	.286	-0.3	3B(2): -0.2	0.1
2021 FS	*NYM*	*MLB*	*21*	*600*	*42*	*.275*	*-0.6*	*3B 0*	*-3.4*

Yoenis Céspedes LF

Born: 10/18/85 Age: 35 Bats: R Throws: R
Height: 5'11" Weight: 225 Origin: International Free Agent, 2012

YEAR	TEAM	LVL	AGE	PA	R	2B	3B	HR	RBI	BB	K	SB	CS	AVG/OBP/SLG
2018	NYM	MLB	32	157	20	6	0	9	29	13	50	3	0	.262/.325/.496
2020	NYM	MLB	34	34	3	1	0	2	4	2	15	0	0	.161/.235/.387
2021 FS	NYM	MLB	35	600	71	25	1	28	83	45	174	3	2	.233/.301/.441

Comparables: Frank Howard, Willie Horton, Alfonso Soriano

Legendary even before he played his first game in America, and so improbable that he may as well have been written by Terry Pratchett, of course *La Potencia* made an unlikely return to the Mets during the bizarre, abbreviated season we all just witnessed. Blessed by the advent of the National League DH, Céspedes took on the role of *Casey at the Bat* for the Amazins, struggling mightily for eight games–but hammering two dingers–before opting out of his return engagement. In a world where every player has been scouted since the womb, and where the reams of performance data drown us in terabytes, Céspedes was the last tall tale. He leaves the Mets, and maybe the major leagues, much the way he came to us: unpredictable, compelling, charismatic, and almost downright fictional.

YEAR	TEAM	LVL	AGE	PA	DRC+	BABIP	BRR	FRAA	WARP
2018	NYM	MLB	32	157	99	.333	0.5	LF(35): 1.8	0.6
2020	NYM	MLB	34	34	75	.214	0.0		0.0
2021 FS	NYM	MLB	35	600	98	.289	-0.6	LF 5, 1B 0	1.8

Pete Crow-Armstrong OF

Born: 03/25/02 Age: 19 Bats: L Throws: L
Height: 6'1" Weight: 180 Origin: Round 1, 2020 Draft (#19 overall)

Crow-Armstrong, a prep center fielder from the prestigious Harvard-Westlake High School in California, is the son of two actors who had recurring roles on the mid-aughts NBC TV series *Heroes*. Rather appropriately, the 19th-overall pick in the 2020 draft has his own superpower: he's already an outstanding defender in center field, with above-average skills across the board, plus speed, and a preternatural ability to read the ball off the bat and run stellar routes. Like with every other prep hitter, the bat will be a question mark until it isn't, and he may never develop even average game power. The hope is that he'll develop into a tremendous defensive asset who hits for average and corks a few line drives over the fence, but we'll either have to wait four years or steal Hiro Nakamura's time travel powers to find out if he'll reach that potential.

Luis Guillorme SS

Born: 09/27/94 Age: 26 Bats: L Throws: R
Height: 5'10" Weight: 190 Origin: Round 10, 2013 Draft (#296 overall)

YEAR	TEAM	LVL	AGE	PA	R	2B	3B	HR	RBI	BB	K	SB	CS	AVG/OBP/SLG
2018	LV	AAA	23	281	41	15	2	3	33	30	39	2	1	.304/.380/.417
2018	NYM	MLB	23	74	4	2	0	0	5	7	3	1	0	.209/.284/.239
2019	SYR	AAA	24	278	33	12	0	7	32	39	42	4	4	.307/.412/.452
2019	NYM	MLB	24	70	8	4	0	1	3	7	14	0	0	.246/.324/.361
2020	NYM	MLB	25	68	6	6	0	0	9	10	17	2	0	.333/.426/.439
2021 FS	NYM	MLB	26	600	71	27	1	9	64	67	119	0	1	.248/.337/.356
2021 DC	NYM	MLB	26	380	45	17	0	5	40	42	75	0	0	.248/.337/.356

Comparables: Gordon Beckham, Bret Barberie, Brent Gates

The most dextrous defender in blue and orange since Rey Ordoñez, Guillorme used his limited 2020 playing time to do something he'd never managed in his previous cups of coffee with the big club: string together more than a handful of hits and post the sort of snazzy batting average that transforms a high-minors depth profile into that of a valuable utility infielder. Perhaps the new Mets regime will value infield defense more than the prior ones, but given the surfeit of bodies on the left side of the infield, Guillorme is likely to find playing time only if he skips town, despite his most impressive all-around season to date.

YEAR	TEAM	LVL	AGE	PA	DRC+	BABIP	BRR	FRAA	WARP
2018	LV	AAA	23	281	106	.350	0.3	SS(54): 1.9, 2B(9): -1.4, 3B(5): 1.0	1.3
2018	NYM	MLB	23	74	92	.219	0.7	3B(14): -1.8, 2B(8): -0.5	0.0
2019	SYR	AAA	24	278	130	.346	0.7	2B(30): -0.3, SS(26): -0.9, 3B(13): 0.1	1.9
2019	NYM	MLB	24	70	85	.304	0.4	2B(8): 0.0, SS(8): -0.2, 3B(5): -0.0	0.2
2020	NYM	MLB	25	68	90	.463	0.0	2B(17): 0.2, 3B(4): -0.3, SS(3): 0.0	0.1
2021 FS	NYM	MLB	26	600	93	.306	-1.0	3B -2, 2B 0	0.8
2021 DC	NYM	MLB	26	380	93	.306	-0.6	3B -1, 2B 0	0.4

Guillermo Heredia CF

Born: 01/31/91 Age: 30 Bats: R Throws: L
Height: 5'10" Weight: 195 Origin: International Free Agent, 2016

YEAR	TEAM	LVL	AGE	PA	R	2B	3B	HR	RBI	BB	K	SB	CS	AVG/OBP/SLG
2018	TAC	AAA	27	37	4	1	0	0	2	4	3	2	1	.286/.432/.321
2018	SEA	MLB	27	337	29	14	1	5	19	32	52	2	4	.236/.318/.342
2019	DUR	AAA	28	30	3	1	0	1	4	1	10	0	1	.214/.267/.357
2019	TB	MLB	28	231	31	13	0	5	20	18	60	2	2	.225/.306/.363
2020	NYM	MLB	29	18	4	0	0	2	3	1	5	0	0	.235/.278/.588
2020	PIT	MLB	29	18	2	0	0	0	2	2	4	1	0	.188/.278/.188
2021 FS	NYM	MLB	30	600	75	26	1	14	70	53	124	4	3	.241/.328/.380

Comparables: Rusty Kuntz, Jeff Barry, Dave Stegman

If archetypal fourth outfielder Heredia was going to find more playing time, the 2020 Pirates outfield seemed like the perfect opportunity. Unfortunately, he didn't even last the short season on the roster and found his way to the best offensive outfield in the majors, paving the way for a 2021 return as—you guessed it—a fourth outfielder.

YEAR	TEAM	LVL	AGE	PA	DRC+	BABIP	BRR	FRAA	WARP
2018	TAC	AAA	27	37	113	.308	0.9	LF(6): 1.0, CF(5): -0.5	0.3
2018	SEA	MLB	27	337	88	.270	0.0	CF(89): -6.5, LF(32): 3.1, RF(2): -0.1	0.3
2019	DUR	AAA	28	30	66	.294	0.0	CF(8): -0.2	0.0
2019	TB	MLB	28	231	76	.293	2.0	CF(41): 0.5, RF(28): 0.8, LF(14): -0.0	0.4
2020	NYM	MLB	29	18	90	.200	-0.1	CF(7): 0.4	0.0
2020	PIT	MLB	29	18	92	.250	-0.1	RF(5): 0.4, CF(2): 0.1	0.3
2021 FS	*NYM*	*MLB*	*30*	*600*	*97*	*.289*	*-0.5*	*CF 0, LF 1*	*1.6*

Khalil Lee CF

Born: 06/26/98 Age: 23 Bats: L Throws: L
Height: 5'10" Weight: 170 Origin: Round 3, 2016 Draft (#103 overall)

YEAR	TEAM	LVL	AGE	PA	R	2B	3B	HR	RBI	BB	K	SB	CS	AVG/OBP/SLG
2018	WIL	HI-A	20	301	42	13	4	4	41	48	75	14	3	.270/.402/.406
2018	NWA	AA	20	118	15	5	0	2	10	11	28	2	2	.245/.330/.353
2019	NWA	AA	21	546	74	21	3	8	51	65	154	53	12	.264/.363/.372
2021 FS	*NYM*	*MLB*	*23*	*600*	*62*	*21*	*4*	*12*	*52*	*56*	*218*	*15*	*7*	*.202/.290/.329*

Comparables: Clint Frazier, Austin Jackson, Luis Alexander Basabe

Is Lee a future everyday player or just a speedy fourth outfielder who'll leave you wanting more? In a kinder parallel universe, Lee may have been given the opportunity to start to answer that question via a full season of at-bats against high-minors pitching. Instead, he spent all of 2020 at the Royals' alternate site, and while reports there were encouraging, they didn't do enough to move the needle. Lee remains an enigma: too talented to fall out of the Royals' top-10 prospects list, but too inconsistent at the plate to enter the true National Prospect Consciousness™. Kansas City liked him enough to add him to the 40-man this winter, but not so much that they refrained from signing Michael A. Taylor to fill the speedy fourth outfielder role.

YEAR	TEAM	LVL	AGE	PA	DRC+	BABIP	BRR	FRAA	WARP
2018	WIL	HI-A	20	301	140	.371	2.2	CF(57): 3.8, RF(9): 0.3	2.2
2018	NWA	AA	20	118	82	.319	0.6	CF(17): 0.3, LF(9): 0.7	0.0
2019	NWA	AA	21	546	117	.374	3.7	RF(55): -6.0, CF(45): -5.7, LF(8): -0.1	1.2
2021 FS	*NYM*	*MLB*	*23*	*600*	*70*	*.317*	*1.5*	*CF 2, RF -1*	*-0.4*

Ronny Mauricio SS
Born: 04/04/01 Age: 20 Bats: S Throws: R
Height: 6'3" Weight: 166 Origin: International Free Agent, 2017

YEAR	TEAM	LVL	AGE	PA	R	2B	3B	HR	RBI	BB	K	SB	CS	AVG/OBP/SLG
2018	MTS	ROK	17	212	26	13	3	3	31	10	31	1	6	.279/.307/.421
2018	KNG	ROK	17	35	6	3	0	0	4	3	9	1	0	.233/.286/.333
2019	COL	LO-A	18	504	62	20	5	4	37	23	99	6	10	.268/.307/.357
2021 FS	NYM	MLB	20	600	44	22	3	7	48	30	168	3	4	.212/.256/.301

Comparables: Cole Tucker, Alcides Escobar, Andrew Velazquez

One of the biggest baseball-related disappointments of 2020 was the loss of the minor-league season. That meant losing out on the opportunity to watch the growth and development of players like Mauricio, who live in that special place far enough away from the majors to never have disappointed us, yet are starting to flash world-class skills that wouldn't be out of place on an All-Star team. Success isn't remotely assured for the rangy shortstop—he'll need to grow into some power and prove his hit tool against tougher pitching—but even after the lost season, he still remains in that sweet spot between "too far away" and "yeah, we know him." There's been a litany of hyped Mets shortstop prospects over the past two decades, but Mauricio still retains the possibility of being the best of the bunch.

YEAR	TEAM	LVL	AGE	PA	DRC+	BABIP	BRR	FRAA	WARP
2018	MTS	ROK	17	212		.310			
2018	KNG	ROK	17	35		.304			
2019	COL	LO-A	18	504	100	.330	2.9	SS(106): -0.1	2.3
2021 FS	NYM	MLB	20	600	51	.289	-0.1	SS 2	-1.8

Eduardo Núñez 2B
Born: 06/15/87 Age: 34 Bats: R Throws: R
Height: 6'0" Weight: 195 Origin: International Free Agent, 2004

YEAR	TEAM	LVL	AGE	PA	R	2B	3B	HR	RBI	BB	K	SB	CS	AVG/OBP/SLG
2018	BOS	MLB	31	502	56	23	3	10	44	16	69	7	2	.265/.289/.388
2019	BOS	MLB	32	174	13	7	0	2	20	4	27	5	1	.228/.243/.305
2020	NYM	MLB	33	2	0	0	0	0	0	0	0	1	0	.500/.500/.500
2021 FS	NYM	MLB	34	600	57	25	1	14	64	27	102	23	8	.253/.293/.382

Comparables: Clete Boyer, Bill Stein, Terry Pendleton

It only took two big-league plate appearances before Núñez's long-standing knee issues hobbled him and brought his season (and likely his career) to a close. Without his signature speed and the defensive flexibility that comes with it, he's likely played the last meaningful major-league game of a solid career.

New York Mets 2021

YEAR	TEAM	LVL	AGE	PA	DRC+	BABIP	BRR	FRAA	WARP
2018	BOS	MLB	31	502	83	.290	-2.6	2B(74): -2.0, 3B(45): 1.2	0.2
2019	BOS	MLB	32	174	58	.257	1.7	2B(31): 1.3, 3B(8): -0.5, SS(6): -0.5	-0.2
2020	NYM	MLB	33	2	96	.500		RF(1): 0.1	0.0
2021 FS	NYM	MLB	34	600	82	.286	1.7	2B -1, 3B -1	0.2

René Rivera C
Born: 07/31/83   Age: 37   Bats: R   Throws: R
Height: 5'10"   Weight: 215   Origin: Round 2, 2001 Draft (#49 overall)

YEAR	TEAM	LVL	AGE	PA	R	2B	3B	HR	RBI	BB	K	SB	CS	AVG/OBP/SLG
2018	IE	HI-A	34	25	4	0	0	2	3	3	5	0	0	.286/.400/.571
2018	LAA	MLB	34	87	8	4	0	4	11	4	32	0	0	.244/.287/.439
2018	ATL	MLB	34	4	0	0	0	0	0	0	3	0	0	.000/.000/.000
2019	SYR	AAA	35	396	53	13	0	25	73	31	103	0	0	.254/.319/.501
2019	NYM	MLB	35	20	2	0	0	1	3	3	4	0	0	.235/.350/.412
2020	NYM	MLB	36	4	0	0	0	0	0	0	3	0	0	.250/.250/.250
2021 FS	NYM	MLB	37	600	67	21	0	27	78	36	209	1	1	.220/.279/.408

Comparables: Tim Laker, Mike Rivera, Sandy Martinez

YEAR	TEAM	P. COUNT	FRM RUNS	BLK RUNS	THRW RUNS	TOT RUNS
2018	ATL	136	0.1	0.2	-0.1	0.2
2018	LAA	3346	1.6	-1.6	0.2	0.1
2019	NYM	858	0.1	-0.7	-0.1	-0.7
2019	SYR	11258	1.4	0.0	3.2	4.5
2020	NYM	135	0.0	0.0	0.0	0.0
2021	NYM	16650	3.3	-1.1	0.6	2.7
2021	NYM	16650	3.3	-4.4	0.6	-0.5

A full 16 years after his MLB debut, veteran backstop Rene Rivera leveraged every team's need for an everyday third catcher into two appearances with the Mets. Unfortunately, his season ended early due to elbow surgery in his non-throwing arm, leaving his status as a preeminent defense-first Triple-A safety valve in jeopardy.

YEAR	TEAM	LVL	AGE	PA	DRC+	BABIP	BRR	FRAA	WARP
2018	IE	HI-A	34	25	131	.286	0.1	C(4): -0.0	0.1
2018	LAA	MLB	34	87	74	.348	-1.1	C(26): 0.5, 1B(2): -0.0	0.1
2018	ATL	MLB	34	4	72	.000		C(3): 0.2	0.0
2019	SYR	AAA	35	396	105	.281	-2.0	C(80): 5.1, 1B(2): -0.1, P(1): -0.0	2.2
2019	NYM	MLB	35	20	90	.250		C(8): -0.6	0.0
2020	NYM	MLB	36	4	89	1.000		C(1): -0.0	0.0
2021 FS	NYM	MLB	37	600	81	.300	-0.9	C -1, 1B 0	0.9

Mallex Smith CF

Born: 05/06/93 Age: 28 Bats: L Throws: R
Height: 5'10" Weight: 180 Origin: Round 5, 2012 Draft (#165 overall)

YEAR	TEAM	LVL	AGE	PA	R	2B	3B	HR	RBI	BB	K	SB	CS	AVG/OBP/SLG
2018	TB	MLB	25	544	65	27	10	2	40	47	98	40	12	.296/.367/.406
2019	TAC	AAA	26	48	8	3	0	1	6	3	4	7	0	.333/.375/.467
2019	SEA	MLB	26	566	70	19	9	6	37	42	140	46	9	.227/.300/.335
2020	SEA	MLB	27	47	2	2	0	0	3	2	13	2	0	.133/.170/.178
2021 FS	NYM	MLB	28	600	53	20	6	8	53	51	146	36	12	.230/.305/.340

Comparables: Cesar Geronimo, Herm Winningham, Cecil Espy

After years and years (and years) of utter developmental failure, the Mariners appear to be turning the corner. Unfortunately, it would appear ending the curse that has plagued Mariner minor leaguers for a decade, scattering them to Japan and to culinary schools, required one final blood sacrifice. Alas, Smith drew the short straw for being tossed into the volcano. The speedy outfielder's game disintegrated; he set career lows in practically every category except errors and saw himself reduced to wandering around the Tacoma intramural expo that served at the minor leagues in 2020. He's still only 28 and a couple years removed from his breakout year in Tampa Bay. When he bounces back to be a productive regular for the Mets in 2021, remember for all that fanbase's kvetching that it turns out the real Mets were the Mariners, all along.

YEAR	TEAM	LVL	AGE	PA	DRC+	BABIP	BRR	FRAA	WARP
2018	TB	MLB	25	544	98	.366	4.4	CF(71): -7.0, RF(47): -1.9, LF(38): -1.2	0.9
2019	TAC	AAA	26	48	107	.350	0.6	CF(10): 0.2	0.3
2019	SEA	MLB	26	566	73	.301	6.8	CF(106): -5.9, RF(28): 2.5, LF(5): 0.0	0.3
2020	SEA	MLB	27	47	63	.188	0.0	RF(12): -1.1, CF(3): -0.2	-0.3
2021 FS	NYM	MLB	28	600	79	.300	3.8	CF -2, RF 1	0.3

Mark Vientos 3B

Born: 12/11/99 Age: 21 Bats: R Throws: R
Height: 6'4" Weight: 185 Origin: Round 2, 2017 Draft (#59 overall)

YEAR	TEAM	LVL	AGE	PA	R	2B	3B	HR	RBI	BB	K	SB	CS	AVG/OBP/SLG
2018	KNG	ROK	18	262	32	12	0	11	52	37	43	1	0	.287/.389/.489
2019	COL	LO-A	19	454	48	27	1	12	62	22	110	1	4	.255/.300/.411
2021 FS	NYM	MLB	21	600	49	22	1	12	54	38	186	0	1	.198/.256/.309

Comparables: Nick Castellanos, Neftali Soto, Rio Ruiz

Even at the age of 20, Vientos can muscle the ball out of a park going the other way and he performed well enough in 2019 to spark visions of a bright future. Filling out and figuring out the holes in his swing are the next steps.

YEAR	TEAM	LVL	AGE	PA	DRC+	BABIP	BRR	FRAA	WARP
2018	KNG	ROK	18	262		.312			
2019	COL	LO-A	19	454	122	.311	-5.2	3B(100): -3.0	1.5
2021 FS	NYM	MLB	21	600	54	.275	-1.0	3B 0	-2.6

Matthew Allan   RHP

Born: 04/17/01   Age: 20   Bats: R   Throws: R
Height: 6'3"   Weight: 225   Origin: Round 3, 2019 Draft (#89 overall)

YEAR	TEAM	LVL	AGE	W	L	SV	G	GS	IP	H	HR	BB/9	K/9	K	GB%	BABIP
2019	MTS	ROK	18	1	0	0	5	4	8¹	5	0	4.3	11.9	11	31.6%	.263
2019	BRK	SS	18	0	0	0	1	1	2	5	0	4.5	13.5	3	42.9%	.714
2021 FS	NYM	MLB	20	2	3	0	57	0	50	47	8	6.0	8.5	47	35.7%	.288

Comparables: Tyler Glasnow, Eduardo Rodriguez, Noah Syndergaard

Instead of spending a full season hewing through Low-A hitters in Columbia or St. Lucie, the Mets' top pitching prospect joined the team's 60-man player pool in the middle of August, returning to the same Brooklyn field where he had such success during the previous season's New York-Penn League playoffs. While Allan was facing the team's other top prospects and a few major-league quality hitters, one of the goals was to convert his changeup from what he previously called a "slow fastball" to a different offering with more break and greater separation from his heater. If he can build up a third plus pitch to go with his fastball and curveball, he'll be facing (and beating) more high-minors hitters by the end of next season.

YEAR	TEAM	LVL	AGE	WHIP	ERA	DRA-	WARP	MPH	FB%	WHF	CSP
2019	MTS	ROK	18	1.08	1.08						
2019	BRK	SS	18	3.00	9.00	136	0.0				
2021 FS	NYM	MLB	20	1.62	5.57	120	-0.3				

Jerad Eickhoff RHP
Born: 07/02/90 Age: 31 Bats: R Throws: R
Height: 6'4" Weight: 246 Origin: Round 15, 2011 Draft (#474 overall)

YEAR	TEAM	LVL	AGE	W	L	SV	G	GS	IP	H	HR	BB/9	K/9	K	GB%	BABIP
2018	CLR	HI-A	27	0	1	0	3	3	9	3	2	4.0	10.0	10	36.8%	.062
2018	LHV	AAA	27	0	0	0	4	4	18²	17	1	3.9	4.8	10	52.5%	.267
2018	PHI	MLB	27	0	1	0	3	1	5¹	10	1	0.0	18.6	11	20.0%	.643
2019	REA	AA	28	0	1	0	2	2	7¹	8	2	3.7	7.4	6	22.7%	.300
2019	LHV	AAA	28	3	1	0	4	4	17¹	13	3	4.2	8.3	16	25.0%	.227
2019	PHI	MLB	28	3	4	1	12	10	58¹	58	18	2.8	7.7	50	35.1%	.260
2021 FS	NYM	MLB	30	2	3	0	57	0	50	51	9	3.4	8.2	45	36.1%	.296

Comparables: Kevin Gausman, Nick Tropeano, Anthony DeSclafani

LeBron to Cleveland, Griffey to Seattle, Odysseus to Ithaca. And after five years in Philadelphia, Eickhoff triumphantly returned to the organization that drafted him, signing with the Rangers midseason. Even if he technically never took the field, 2020 wasn't a total loss; after serving up a home run on nearly a quarter of his fly balls in 2019, it had to be comforting to watch so many snagged at the warning track at Globe Life Field. Eickhoff has since joined the Mets, ending his Texas reunion with a whimper.

YEAR	TEAM	LVL	AGE	WHIP	ERA	DRA-	WARP	MPH	FB%	WHF	CSP
2018	CLR	HI-A	27	0.78	3.00	70	0.2				
2018	LHV	AAA	27	1.34	2.41	99	0.1				
2018	PHI	MLB	27	1.88	6.75	68	0.1	92.0	52.0%	42.2%	
2019	REA	AA	28	1.50	9.82	119	-0.1				
2019	LHV	AAA	28	1.21	4.67	85	0.4				
2019	PHI	MLB	28	1.30	5.71	125	-0.3	91.2	39.1%	26.7%	
2021 FS	NYM	MLB	30	1.40	4.91	111	-0.1	91.2	39.7%	27.4%	47.9%

J.T. Ginn RHP
Born: 05/20/99 Age: 22 Bats: R Throws: R
Height: 6'2" Weight: 200 Origin: Round 2, 2020 Draft (#52 overall)

Usually a Mets pitcher experiences a severe elbow injury after they make it to the big leagues, but this time perhaps the team is skipping to the middle of the story instead of starting on page one? Ginn turned down an overslot offer from the Dodgers back in the first round of the 2018 draft, and despite the elbow injury sustained during his second year at Mississippi State, the decision has turned out to make good financial sense for the former SEC Freshman of the Year. The Mets bet big on his ability to rebound from surgery to reclaim his lively fastball and ripping slider, but the early returns on this investment might not be clear until 2022.

Ariel Jurado RHP

Born: 01/30/96 Age: 25 Bats: R Throws: R
Height: 6'2" Weight: 240 Origin: International Free Agent, 2002

YEAR	TEAM	LVL	AGE	W	L	SV	G	GS	IP	H	HR	BB/9	K/9	K	GB%	BABIP
2018	FRI	AA	22	5	3	0	16	16	101^2	107	12	1.5	5.1	58	51.0%	.291
2018	TEX	MLB	22	5	5	0	12	8	54^2	66	7	3.0	3.5	21	51.7%	.304
2019	NAS	AAA	23	3	0	0	4	4	22^2	29	1	0.8	8.7	22	38.0%	.400
2019	TEX	MLB	23	7	11	0	32	18	122^1	148	21	2.6	6.0	81	46.0%	.322
2020	NYM	MLB	24	0	0	0	1	1	4	9	1	0.0	4.5	2	31.6%	.471
2021 FS	*NYM*	*MLB*	*25*	*2*	*3*	*0*	*57*	*0*	*50*	*55*	*9*	*2.6*	*6.2*	*34*	*45.6%*	*.294*

Comparables: Antonio Senzatela, Sean Reid-Foley, Zach Eflin

After eight years in the Rangers' system, Texas finally gave up on the swing-starter and former top prospect. After getting dealt to the Mets, Jurado made one terribly ill-fated start before setting out in search of the third organization of his career.

YEAR	TEAM	LVL	AGE	WHIP	ERA	DRA-	WARP	MPH	FB%	WHF	CSP
2018	FRI	AA	22	1.22	3.28	126	-1.0				
2018	TEX	MLB	22	1.54	5.93	155	-1.1	93.3	70.4%	10.4%	
2019	NAS	AAA	23	1.37	3.57	99	0.4				
2019	TEX	MLB	23	1.50	5.81	147	-2.0	94.2	64.2%	18.1%	
2020	NYM	MLB	24	2.25	11.25	110	0.0	93.2	50.0%	22.0%	
2021 FS	*NYM*	*MLB*	*25*	*1.39*	*5.01*	*112*	*-0.1*	*94.0*	*64.5%*	*17.0%*	*49.0%*

Mike Montgomery LHP

Born: 07/01/89 Age: 32 Bats: L Throws: L
Height: 6'5" Weight: 220 Origin: Round 1, 2008 Draft (#36 overall)

YEAR	TEAM	LVL	AGE	W	L	SV	G	GS	IP	H	HR	BB/9	K/9	K	GB%	BABIP
2018	CHC	MLB	28	5	6	0	38	19	124	131	10	2.8	6.2	86	50.5%	.311
2019	IOW	AAA	29	1	1	0	2	2	10	3	0	3.6	7.2	8	55.6%	.111
2019	KC	MLB	29	2	7	0	13	13	64	78	12	3.0	7.2	51	50.7%	.349
2019	CHC	MLB	29	1	2	0	20	0	27	35	6	4.3	6.0	18	42.4%	.345
2020	KC	MLB	30	0	0	0	3	1	5[1]	6	1	1.7	6.8	4	55.6%	.294
2021 FS	NYM	MLB	31	2	3	0	57	0	50	51	6	3.6	7.6	42	50.2%	.301

Comparables: Erasmo Ramírez, Drew Pomeranz, Neil Ramírez

When Montgomery was acquired from the Cubs in July of 2019, one couldn't help but think he was a placeholder. Under club control until after the 2021 season, he could use his five-pitch arsenal to shore up the rotation and eat a modest amount of innings. However one man's injury is another man's opportunity and when Montgomery was sidelined with a lat strain after his first appearance in 2020, it opened the door for Kris Bubic to step forward in the rotation. Outrighted to the minors following the season, he refused the assignment and elected free agency. It looks like the Royals didn't need a placeholder after all.

YEAR	TEAM	LVL	AGE	WHIP	ERA	DRA-	WARP	MPH	FB%	WHF	CSP
2018	CHC	MLB	28	1.37	3.99	102	0.9	93.4	49.6%	21.6%	
2019	IOW	AAA	29	0.70	2.70	34	0.5				
2019	KC	MLB	29	1.55	4.64	146	-1.0	93.3	39.9%	22.3%	
2019	CHC	MLB	29	1.78	5.67	181	-0.9	94.5	47.4%	21.0%	
2020	KC	MLB	30	1.31	5.06	105	0.0	91.3	37.1%	19.0%	
2021 FS	NYM	MLB	31	1.43	4.64	107	0.0	93.6	44.6%	21.6%	45.1%

Marcus Stroman   RHP

Born: 05/01/91   Age: 30   Bats: R   Throws: R
Height: 5'7"   Weight: 180   Origin: Round 1, 2012 Draft (#22 overall)

YEAR	TEAM	LVL	AGE	W	L	SV	G	GS	IP	H	HR	BB/9	K/9	K	GB%	BABIP
2018	TOR	MLB	27	4	9	0	19	19	102^1	115	9	3.2	6.8	77	62.6%	.328
2019	TOR	MLB	28	6	11	0	21	21	124^2	118	10	2.5	7.1	99	54.8%	.293
2019	NYM	MLB	28	4	2	0	11	11	59^2	65	8	3.5	9.1	60	48.0%	.339
2021 FS	NYM	MLB	30	9	8	0	26	26	150	147	20	3.4	8.1	135	54.1%	.298
2021 DC	NYM	MLB	30	9	8	0	25	25	142.3	140	19	3.4	8.1	128	54.1%	.298

Comparables: Sonny Gray, Kevin Gausman, Kyle Hendricks

Already dealing with a torn calf muscle, Stroman made the choice to opt out of the 2020 season, dealing a serious blow to the Mets' already-thin rotation. His second important choice of the calendar year, the decision to accept the team's qualifying offer of $18.9 million and return for the 2021 season, was just as surprising but much more welcome for the Flushing Faithful. Stroman's sinker-slider-cutter pitch mix isn't a perfect fit for the Mets' unexceptional infield defense, but his attitude towards the club—including an enthusiastic approval of new owner Steve Cohen—and New York roots make him a logical fit in Queens. Given that the Mets rotation tends towards the extremes: the highs of deGrom and Syndergaard and the lows of ... most everybody else, Stroman's solid third-starter profile is a most welcome return.

YEAR	TEAM	LVL	AGE	WHIP	ERA	DRA-	WARP	MPH	FB%	WHF	CSP
2018	TOR	MLB	27	1.48	5.54	93	1.3	93.7	49.3%	22.4%	
2019	TOR	MLB	28	1.23	2.96	76	2.8	93.9	36.9%	24.2%	
2019	NYM	MLB	28	1.47	3.77	79	1.2	93.4	44.1%	25.5%	
2021 FS	NYM	MLB	30	1.36	4.16	95	1.9	93.7	41.5%	24.2%	45.3%
2021 DC	NYM	MLB	30	1.36	4.16	95	1.8	93.7	41.5%	24.2%	45.3%

Noah Syndergaard   RHP

Born: 08/29/92   Age: 28   Bats: L   Throws: R
Height: 6'6"   Weight: 242   Origin: Round 1, 2010 Draft (#38 overall)

YEAR	TEAM	LVL	AGE	W	L	SV	G	GS	IP	H	HR	BB/9	K/9	K	GB%	BABIP
2018	NYM	MLB	25	13	4	0	25	25	154^1	148	9	2.3	9.0	155	48.5%	.323
2019	NYM	MLB	26	10	8	0	32	32	197^2	194	24	2.3	9.2	202	47.3%	.315
2021 FS	NYM	MLB	28	10	7	0	26	26	150	135	17	2.6	9.7	161	47.1%	.300
2021 DC	NYM	MLB	28	5	4	0	19	16	81	73	9	2.6	9.7	87	47.1%	.300

Comparables: Stephen Strasburg, Aaron Nola, Clayton Kershaw

Try to imagine what it's like to have ulnar collateral ligament surgery, the kind that cost Syndergaard his season. It's the middle of March, 2020. You've found out that, though no fault of your own, so much of your world is about to change abruptly. Your health has to be a primary focus, and you'll spend the next several months poring over every small change in feeling, hoping that it's not a sign something went wrong. Time will slow down, and you'll become physically limited in what you can or can't do. Your normal routines will break down, and you may even find yourself with odd pockets of spare time and no idea what to do with it. You'll become physically disconnected from your co-workers and/or friends, people you're used to spending time with on a regular basis. There's pain, and boredom, and work, but eventually a light at the end of the tunnel. Summer 2021. There's a chance that things could go back to some kind of normal. It may not be exactly the same; it may take some time to get back to where you were. Maybe it won't work out. Maybe things could even get better. Can you imagine it?

YEAR	TEAM	LVL	AGE	WHIP	ERA	DRA-	WARP	MPH	FB%	WHF	CSP
2018	NYM	MLB	25	1.21	3.03	55	5.0	99.3	53.7%	28.4%	
2019	NYM	MLB	26	1.23	4.28	69	5.1	99.3	59.2%	27.0%	
2021 FS	NYM	MLB	28	1.19	3.26	78	3.3	99.3	57.6%	27.4%	49.3%
2021 DC	NYM	MLB	28	1.19	3.26	78	1.8	99.3	57.6%	27.4%	49.3%

Thomas Szapucki LHP

Born: 06/12/96 Age: 25 Bats: R Throws: L
Height: 6'2" Weight: 181 Origin: Round 5, 2015 Draft (#149 overall)

YEAR	TEAM	LVL	AGE	W	L	SV	G	GS	IP	H	HR	BB/9	K/9	K	GB%	BABIP
2019	COL	LO-A	23	0	0	0	11	8	21²	14	1	4.2	10.8	26	33.3%	.260
2019	STL	HI-A	23	1	3	0	9	9	36	33	1	3.8	10.5	42	48.5%	.337
2021 FS	NYM	MLB	25	2	3	0	57	0	50	45	7	4.9	9.0	50	38.8%	.284
2021 DC	NYM	MLB	25	0	0	0	14	0	11.3	10	1	4.9	9.0	11	38.8%	.284

Comparables: Domingo Germán, Alex Reyes, John Gant

Instead of getting a clear picture of what post-Tommy John life might be like for Szapucki after a taste of facing upper-minors bats, the one-time top prospect faced another delay in a career already chock full of them. While somewhat effective in his 2019 stint in the low minors, it's entirely possible that his stuff will never return to the heights he flashed back in 2016. Maybe 2021 will finally be the show-me year for the star-crossed southpaw: either he'll be able to build up enough arm strength to remain a solid starting pitching prospect, or it will be time to downshift him into a bullpen role.

YEAR	TEAM	LVL	AGE	WHIP	ERA	DRA-	WARP	MPH	FB%	WHF	CSP
2019	COL	LO-A	23	1.11	2.08	74	0.4				
2019	STL	HI-A	23	1.33	3.25	96	0.1				
2021 FS	NYM	MLB	25	1.45	4.67	105	0.1				
2021 DC	NYM	MLB	25	1.45	4.67	105	0.0				

Nick Tropeano RHP
Born: 08/27/90 Age: 30 Bats: R Throws: R
Height: 6'4" Weight: 205 Origin: Round 5, 2011 Draft (#160 overall)

YEAR	TEAM	LVL	AGE	W	L	SV	G	GS	IP	H	HR	BB/9	K/9	K	GB%	BABIP
2018	IE	HI-A	27	1	1	0	2	2	9	9	1	1.0	9.0	9	26.9%	.320
2018	LAA	MLB	27	5	6	0	14	14	76	68	16	3.7	7.6	64	37.9%	.256
2019	SL	AAA	28	4	6	0	17	15	79^2	90	12	3.5	9.6	85	34.6%	.351
2019	LAA	MLB	28	0	1	0	3	1	13^2	18	6	4.0	6.6	10	25.0%	.286
2020	PIT	MLB	29	1	0	0	7	0	15^2	14	1	2.3	10.9	19	29.3%	.325
2021 FS	NYM	MLB	30	2	2	0	57	0	50	46	9	3.8	9.2	50	33.9%	.285

Comparables: Kevin Gausman, Jake Odorizzi, Dan Straily

After escaping the Angels' pitching ranks and sheltering for a while among the Yankees' reserves, Tropeano was plucked from the waiver wire by the Pirates and proceeded to have his best season as a pro. Pittsburgh encouraged him to throw his split finger more than ever before, resulting in him almost doubling his strikeout percentage from last season. While initially picked up to cover innings after Joe Musgrove's injury, Tropeano pitched effectively out of the bullpen as a long reliever for Pittsburgh's mercurial pitching staff. After being waived and non-tendered in a single weary autumn, he'll enter 2021 forced to prove himself all over again, this time with the Mets.

YEAR	TEAM	LVL	AGE	WHIP	ERA	DRA-	WARP	MPH	FB%	WHF	CSP
2018	IE	HI-A	27	1.11	2.00	59	0.2				
2018	LAA	MLB	27	1.30	4.74	106	0.5	92.0	47.5%	27.4%	
2019	SL	AAA	28	1.52	5.87	87	1.9				
2019	LAA	MLB	28	1.76	9.88	187	-0.5	92.2	46.5%	27.0%	
2020	PIT	MLB	29	1.15	1.15	89	0.2	92.2	30.2%	33.3%	
2021 FS	NYM	MLB	30	1.36	4.60	103	0.2	92.1	42.1%	29.1%	45.5%

Mets Prospects

The State of the System:
The Mets' new ownership and front office will have to do a fair bit of work to build out a very shallow system, but aggressive moves at the top of the last two drafts mean the cupboard isn't completely bare.

The Top Ten:

1

★ ★ ★ *2021 Top 101 Prospect* **#42** ★ ★ ★

Ronny Mauricio   SS   OFP: 60   ETA: Late-2022
Born: 04/04/01   Age: 20   Bats: S   Throws: R   Height: 6'3"   Weight: 166
Origin: International Free Agent, 2017

The Report: Mauricio was aggressively sent to the South Atlantic League in 2019, making his full-season debut on his 18th birthday. He didn't exactly shine there statistically, but he held his own given his age. His hit tool plays as a potential plus, with good feel for hitting and plus bat speed. His game power is theoretical at present, but he has above-average-to-plus raw and could get there in games with further physical development and additional loft in his swing. Both his hit tool and power are currently limited in games by his aggressiveness at the plate; he walked less than five percent of the time in 2019. Defensively, Mauricio currently has the range for shortstop, with an obvious third base fallback if he grows off the position. There is still a lot of projection here, so there are several different forms his ultimate MLB profile could take.

Development Track: Mauricio was brought to the alternate site in mid-August. He struggled there against more advanced pitching than he was ready for, although his abilities still flashed well. Mets fall instructs were cut short, so he didn't have a major opportunity to rebound there. We're holding his report largely steady since we don't have a ton to go on, honestly; what information we have suggests that he was about where he would've been had he played 2020 as a teenager in High-A as expected.

Variance: High. A year of lost reps at 19 probably isn't great here, and we're optimistic he gets on track in 2021.

Mark Barry's Fantasy Take: The promise of a little extra pop in Mauricio's stick is nice, but honestly, you had me at the potentially plus hit tool. There's very little chance you're getting steals from Mauricio, as he's been thrown out twice as often as he has been successful, but at peak he's a four-category contributor. As it stands now, I'd have him in the top-40ish range for dynasty prospects.

★ ★ ★ *2021 Top 101 Prospect* **#79** ★ ★ ★

2. Matthew Allan   RHP   OFP: 60   ETA: Late 2022 / Early 2023
Born: 04/17/01   Age: 20   Bats: R   Throws: R   Height: 6'3"   Weight: 225
Origin: Round 3, 2019 Draft (#89 overall)

The Report: Allan was a first-round talent in the 2019 draft who slipped to the third reportedly because of bonus demands. The Mets scraped together $2.5 million, picking almost entirely under-slot senior signs after him to make the money work. It sure looks like it's paying early dividends. Allan showed mid-90s heat and a potential plus curveball in the complex and at Coney Island, and the pitchability and command were advanced for a teenaged arm. His 6-foot-3, 225-lb. frame is functionally the ideal size for a pitching prospect and there's no concerning markers in his delivery. The only real quibbles you could have with Allan coming into 2020 is the changeup needed work—although, again less so compared to most of his cohort—he hadn't pitched a full pro season, and the track record of non-elite righty prep arms is a lot more noise than signal.

Development Track: Allan spent about a month at the Mets' alternate site in Brooklyn, then a little less than that at instructs. When on the mound, he showed a little more top-end velocity and big spin rates on both his fastball and curveball. Without a 2020 season, the same quibbles remain, but the stuff is getting harder to ignore. Arms of this quality dictate their own time table, and while I'd expect Allan to start the season in Low-A St. Lucie, he might be back on the beaches of Kings County before the water is warm enough to take a dip.

Variance: High. All the usual young pitching prospect concerns here. Limited pro track record, command and change need grade jumps, generic injury risk. Conversely he's one good, healthy year with moderate improvements in the profile from potential being a Top 50 prospect in baseball. That happens to 20-year-old arms with this kind of stuff, too.

Mark Barry's Fantasy Take: We were all robbed of something in 2020, but dynasty-wise, it's not hard to envision Allan putting up a dominant performance in A-ball and shooting up prospect lists across the industry. The fact that it didn't happen, while bad for his publicist, is good for dynasty managers, as there's still some time to get in on a high-upside prep arm before he takes off (or, you know, before he falls apart because pitchers). The risks are evergreen, but his ceiling makes Allan an interesting gamble.

★ ★ ★ *2021 Top 101 Prospect* **#84** ★ ★ ★

3 **Francisco Alvarez** C   OFP: 60   ETA: 2024
Born: 11/19/01   Age: 19   Bats: R   Throws: R   Height: 5'11"   Weight: 220
Origin: International Free Agent, 2018

The Report: If you've got two recent big ticket IFAs with 60 OFPs in your top three, you've done pretty well in your international scouting department. Alvarez is a power-over-hit prospect offensively, driven by great bat speed and strength. Unlike Mauricio, his power has already shown up in games. The hit tool isn't bad either, and it's buoyed by an advanced plate approach for his age. We're not 100 percent sure he's going to stick at catcher, but all of the signs are positive; he's looked like a good receiver with an above-average arm so far. If the rigors of catching don't cause him to stagnate, he has a chance to be a very good player in a few years time.

Development Track: Alvarez is down a spot on this list, but don't mistake that for us being down on him. His stock is actually slightly up, it's just that Allan's stock is up more. Alvarez performed well at the alternate site after being added around the same time as the prior two players. He tweaked his swing to try and tap into even more power, and got some catching time in. Given that short-season would've been a reasonable 2020 assignment anyway, we don't think much developmental time was lost for him, either.

Variance: Extreme. He's a teenage catcher who hasn't played above rookie ball yet.

Mark Barry's Fantasy Take: I remember 2019. It was a simpler time. I hung out with people. My favorite team wasn't on the verge of trading its best player *(Ed. Note: Cleveland)*. And I still believed in catching prospects. I'm not here to question your beliefs. If you're still a compiler of dynasty catchers, that's fine, and Alvarez is definitely one of your better options. He's just really far away and probably won't see returns for another 3-4 seasons, so be patient.

4 **Pete Crow-Armstrong** OF   OFP: 55   ETA: 2024
Born: 03/25/02   Age: 19   Bats: L   Throws: L   Height: 6'1"   Weight: 180
Origin: Round 1, 2020 Draft (#19 overall)

The Report: Playing at one of the premiere baseball factory high schools in the country, PCA was an early add to the "follow list" for area scouts in southern California. He uses his feet to his benefit in every facet of the game, whether it's ranging in center field where his advanced glove is evident, or putting the ball in play and letting the wheels take over. It's a contact-oriented approach with the main question about his future being his eventual game power: Will it be too much of a line-drive swing resulting in below-average pop? Or can added muscle help with lift in the bat path?

Development Track: His draft stock was back on the upswing following an up-and-down three years that unfairly hyped him as a top-5 pick and then just as unfairly saw the pendulum swing the opposite way. There were flashes in the spring that the regular doubles and triples were turning into the four-bagger variety of extra base hits, something that will continue to hang over him as he gets into pro ball. His lean body keeps him fleet of foot, so adding too much weight might sacrifice his greatest asset.

Variance: High. There is a lot of belief that the bat will come along eventually. Relying so much on his glove and speed, finding a way to impact the game in other ways will not only improve the variance but also vault his OFP upwards. If not, then he's a bench player reserved for specific roles.

Mark Barry's Fantasy Take: The fantasy perception of PCA will rest with his power. If he can provide some pop, he'll be a top-50 guy in short order. That's not to say he'll get there, however. If the bat doesn't really develop he'd be relegated to a role as a speedy defensive replacement or fourth outfielder, good for a handful of steals for your fantasy fortune, but not much else.

5. Brett Baty 3B   OFP: 55   ETA: 2023
Born: 11/13/99   Age: 21   Bats: L   Throws: R   Height: 6'3"   Weight: 210
Origin: Round 1, 2019 Draft (#12 overall)

The Report: Baty was picked in the top half of the first round on the strength of his bat, and the Texan projects as a middle-of-the-order slugger if the offense continues to develop. Baty's approach and plate discipline are advanced, and he already shows plus power to all fields in-game. While the body is already leaning a bit first base-ish and maybe he's not as smooth as you'd like at the hot corner, he's fine at third for now and the arm's strong enough for the left side. Baty can put a real sting into a baseball, but so far he's struggled to make consistent contact against high-level pitching. He drives the ball well the other way, but doesn't always turn around some of the better fastballs he sees.

Development Track: Baty's *raison d'etre* as he enters full season ball will be refining the hit tool so that the patience and power really play, and making sure he remains at third so that the value of these things plays up. So he's still got most of the ladder to climb.

Variance: High. He hasn't yet played full-season ball and the hit tool that should be his calling card hasn't yet solidified.

Mark Barry's Fantasy Take: For dynasty, Baty is probably the second-best prospect in the system. He still has work to do, sure, but the bat is projectable and for our purposes, it really doesn't matter whether he plays first base or third base (or, what the hell, left field—shout out Dom Smith).

6 **J.T. Ginn   RHP**   OFP: 55   ETA: 2024
Born: 05/20/99   Age: 22   Bats: R   Throws: R   Height: 6'2"   Weight: 200
Origin: Round 2, 2020 Draft (#52 overall)

The Report: Originally drafted in the first round by the Dodgers in 2018, Ginn opted to go to Mississippi State and bet on himself for a bigger payday. Following a very strong freshman season for the Bulldogs, he was primed and ready for a breakout season as a draft-eligible sophomore. That season was even shorter than most this past spring, as Ginn needed Tommy John surgery after only one start. When healthy, he possesses one of the best fastballs around because of its elite movement. Still pumping in the low-to-mid 90s, he can locate to either side with arm-side run reminiscent of a Wiffle ball. The secondaries could use some work, with both a slider and changeup lagging behind the quality of the heater.

Development Track: Ginn will enter spring training nearly a year removed from reconstructive elbow surgery, so there will be no rush to get him into games until the Mets believe he's fully capable. There is some reliever risk to the profile, so maybe it wouldn't be the worst thing to build him up through a bullpen role in 2021 before lengthening him back out.

Variance: High. As good as modern elbow surgeries have become, recovery is still different for everyone. Second, there was bullpen-role risk even before the injury It's wait-and-see until he steps on the field.

Mark Barry's Fantasy Take: If there's room on your roster to stash Ginn, I'd take a flier on the talent and pre-TJ stuff. If not, he's a watchlist candidate, for sure, keeping a special eye on how his secondaries come back post-surgery.

7 **Mark Vientos   3B**   OFP: 55   ETA: 2022
Born: 12/11/99   Age: 21   Bats: R   Throws: R   Height: 6'4"   Weight: 185
Origin: Round 2, 2017 Draft (#59 overall)

The Report: The profile on Vientos is actually pretty similar to Baty's, just with less pedigree and an approach at the plate that's not quite as advanced. Though he's lean with some physical projection remaining, Vientos shows plus power to all fields; if there's a tool that will pave his path forward it's the pop. The third base defense is average but he should be able to stay there. The swing is a bit long and the hit tool will be, as it often is, the determining factor here.

Development Track: Wherever 2021 finds him, Vientos will be looking to improve his contact rate, and a bump in plate discipline wouldn't hurt either. How far he goes next year and beyond will be contingent on this. Whatever happens, he's still got a ways to go.

Variance: High. There's uncertainty in the hit tool and he hasn't played above Low-A.

Mark Barry's Fantasy Take: I wish Vientos would strike out less. Sitting down to strikes a quarter of the time in A-ball is not something that particularly bodes well for the future. Still, there's some power in the bat, and I'd be willing to roll the dice in deeper leagues. As it stands not, Vientos is probably a fringe-top-150 dude.

8. Josh Wolf   RHP   OFP: 55   ETA: 2023
Born: 09/01/00   Age: 20   Bats: R   Throws: R   Height: 6'3"   Weight: 170
Origin: Round 2, 2019 Draft (#53 overall)

The Report: Wolf comes right out of central casting for a projectable second-round Texas prep arm. A lean 6-foot-3 with a velocity spike his draft year, Wolf projects to sit mid-90s as he fills out and adds strength in his 20s. The second pitch is a big downer curve. He was drafted as a two-pitch power arm who was a ways off from that projection—which is the difference between first-round Texas prep arms and second-round Texas prep arms, generally speaking—but Wolf injected some upside into an organization that badly needed it on the pitching side.

Development Track: As already mentioned, the Mets were very conservative with regards to bringing non-40-man prospects to the alternate site. Wolf threw at instructs where the reports were uneven, but given the nature of the 2020 "season" we're generally giving a pass to guys where that's the case. 2021 will be an important year for his development, which is boilerplate language for our lists at this point, but still holds true for a lot of 2019 draftees.

Variance: High. Functionally everything that applies to Allan also applies to Wolf. There's also more reliever/durability risk.

Mark Barry's Fantasy Take: There was this FIFA World Cup video game (in, I wanna say, 2006) where the pre-programmed commentary would get awfully excited about an American named Wolf, breaking through the defense to goal. There wasn't much to it, just a supremely English gentleman screaming "WOLF" at the top of his lungs. At the time, my roommate and I found it extremely funny and would yell "Wolf" at each other a lot. Anyway, Mets Wolf is a high-upside dude with only two pitches at present. Right now it's watchlist stuff for me, but I hope he hits so I can scream "WOLF" at the top of my lungs and be the only one that thinks it's funny.

9. Isaiah Greene   OFP: 50   ETA: 2025
Born: 08/29/01   Age: 19   Bats: L   Throws: L   Height: 6'1"   Weight: 180
Origin: Round 2, 2020 Draft (#69 overall)

The Report: With a shortened draft and equally short evaluation period, there were bound to be numerous surprises, and you can mark Greene's selection prior to the third round as one such revelation. He performed very well in stints, flashing some pop as a natural low-ball hitter thanks to his trebuchet of a swing. It's a bit whippy with his hands and wrists twisting at load with a long follow-through. The swing is inefficient at present but despite the length Greene has some feel for the barrel. There is plenty of fluidity in his movements as a plus runner and he should be able to compete for reps with PCA in center field.

Development Track: It certainly is a high variance profile due to the questions about what becomes of the swing. Given that they were both high-pick prep center fielders by the Mets, there will naturally be comparisons between Greene and Crow-Armstrong. Whereas PCA has a longer track record of hitting, Greene may have the better power potential. In the latter's case, finding a consistent launch point and carrying that into games will be pivotal as he receives pro hitting instruction.

Variance: Extreme. The thing about selecting high variance high schoolers in a pandemic-rattled year is that they lose out on all the time that could have been spent tightening up areas of needed focus. It may be a slow start professionally while he works to adjust to everything new being thrown at him.

Mark Barry's Fantasy Take: Plus runner, you say? As the villainous Leonardo Dicaprio said in *Django Unchained*, you had my curiosity, now you have my attention. There's still a long time before that speed will translate to steals for your fantasy roster, but Greene is a sneaky-good name to keep an eye on after the usual suspects in your first-year player drafts.

10 Jaylen Palmer   3B   OFP: 50   ETA: 2024
Born: 07/31/00   Age: 20   Bats: R   Throws: R   Height: 6'3"   Weight: 195
Origin: Round 22, 2018 Draft (#650 overall)

The Report: The Wilpon-era Mets loved a local kid, and Flushing's own Jaylen Palmer went to high school less than five miles from Citi Field. A high school growth spurt has left him a very projectable 6-foot-3 with already present plus raw pop. As he fills out you'd expect him to move off shortstop—he was already splitting time at third in the Appy—but he has the ranginess and arm to fit well at a number of spots in both the infield and outfield. The swing has some length to it, and he struggled with better spin even in rookie ball, so there's not much of a floor to the hit tool. But conversely you could argue he's got the most upside in the system as he could end up with plus game power with the ability to be average-or-better at multiple defensive spots. Palmer is a long way off from those heady heights, though.

Development Track: And of course he didn't get much closer to it in 2020. Palmer could have really used day-in and day-out reps in A-ball to get more comfortable seeing better velocity and secondaries. He spent some time at instructs, working on multiple defensive spots—I posited last year he'd be an intriguing center field prospect, and still think that holds true—but we won't have a good feel for how he's developing until 2021 game action. He functionally moves up on system attrition.

Variance: Extreme. Palmer has made real gains as a pro, but this is still mostly a projection bet. Two years from now he could be a Top 101 prospect, or have stalled out in A-ball.

Mark Barry's Fantasy Take: Oh lovely, two years away from a top-101 spot, which means he's two years away from being two years away from a spot in your fantasy lineup (it was clunky, but I sure do love the "two years away from being two years away" reasoning from Fran Fraschilla). Let's make a pact to meet back here in two years to figure out what we should do with Palmer.

The Prospects You Meet Outside The Top Ten

MLB-arms, but probably relievers

Franklyn Kilome RHP Born: 06/25/95 Age: 26 Bats: R Throws: R Height: 6'6" Weight: 175 Origin: International Free Agent, 2013

Kilomé missed all of 2019 with Tommy John surgery. The Mets used him as an up-and-down depth arm in 2020, and he flashed the former Top 101 form from when he was in the Phillies system in glimpses while also getting shelled in general. Kilomé's been inconsistent with his command and velocity going back a long time now—one of the first things I wrote at BP was about his inconsistency from start-to-start and even inning-to-inning, and I've been here five years now. As a starter, he's probably no more than a back-end arm, and we'd really like to see him air it out with the fastball, which is sometimes mid-90s and touching higher, and the breaking ball, which we've had a plus projection on forever.

Sam McWilliams RHP Born: 09/04/95 Age: 25 Bats: R Throws: R Height: 6'7" Weight: 230 Origin: Round 8, 2014 Draft (#232 overall)

It's highly unusual to find a minor league free agent on a prospect list. The shallowness of this system has a lot to do with that, but McWilliams also wasn't your average MiLB FA. The Mets gave him a major league deal worth $750,000 to win a bidding war for the tall righty. He's been used as a starter for almost his entire minor league career, but a velocity bump into the upper-90s at the Rays alternate site makes him a logical candidate for the Mets 2021 pen. He could have substantial impact in that role, but the real impact might be the signal that the organization is getting more creative in acquiring talent. That will hopefully lead to the next McWilliams not being roughly the 13th-best prospect in the system.

Prospects to dream on a little

Freddy Valdez RF Born: 12/06/01 Age: 19 Bats: R Throws: R Height: 6'3" Weight: 212 Origin: International Free Agent, 2018

Valdez made last season's Mets list thanks in large part to the seven-figure bonus he got in 2018 and a scarcity of system depth. He's made this year's list as well, and I would be engaging in deceit if I were to tell you these factors weren't still at play. He did show promise in the Instructional League, and the fog surrounding his skill set is beginning to lift just a bit. 6-foot-3 and north of 200 lbs, the (just turned) 19-year-old really drives the ball and power-hitting right-fielder is the projection, but a realization of this potential is still beyond the horizon and contingent on what his hit tool looks like in full-season ball.

Alexander Ramírez   Born: 01/13/03   Age: 18   Bats: R   Throws: R   Height: 6'3"   Weight: 170   Origin: International Free Agent, 2019
Ramírez also signed for seven figures, inking a bonus above $2 million in 2019. The 17-year-old outfielder is strong defensively, plays a well-rounded game, and is already showing a bit of pop. As with Valdez, we'll have to see how the hit tool shows as he climbs the ladder and how well the power plays in-game.

Robert Domínguez   RHP   Born: 11/30/01   Age: 19   Bats: R   Throws: R   Height: 6'5"   Weight: 195   Origin: International Free Agent, 2019
At 6-foot-5, 200 lbs, the 19-year-old Domínguez has what you might call a prototypical pitcher's frame. He also has a big right arm, popping the upper-90s consistently and touching triple digits with his fastball while showing secondary stuff and pitching sensibilities that are advanced for his age. There is naturally quite a bit of buzz around the 2019 signee, certainly more than is typical for an over-aged IFA who signed for five figures. There is stuff to dream on here, but also much that is yet to be revealed. We should have a better grasp of his command and control profile, for instance, once we get to see him face live competition.

Top Talents 25 and Under (as of 4/1/2021):

1. Dominic Smith, 1B/OF
2. Andres Gimenez, SS
3. Amed Rosario, SS
4. Ronny Mauricio, SS
5. Matthew Allan, RHP
6. Francisco Alvarez, C
7. Pete Crow-Armstrong, OF
8. Brett Baty, 3B
9. David Peterson, LHP
10. J.T. Ginn, RHP

This was one of the weirder 25U lists to place the MLB talent on—and I watch nearly every game of this team. Dominic Smith is on the verge of stardom, having already turned into a very good MLB hitter with surprising defensive versatility. He's hit .299/.366/.571 with 21 homers over 396 plate appearances stretching over 2019 and 2020, and he got well-deserved down-ballot MVP consideration in

2020. While he will never be a good defender in the outfield, he's worked like hell to become playable in left in a part-time role, and that's let the Mets get his bat in the lineup more.

Andrés Giménez and Amed Rosario feel like two ships passing in the night. Rosario was 2017's No. 7 overall prospect, and might've ranked even higher in 2018 if he hadn't graduated by a few weeks. But he's never consistently hit in the majors—he's just not able to put together good enough at-bats—and his glove at short has been disappointing as well, leading to talk of a move to third or center.

That opened the door for Giménez, who had fallen from No. 38 on our 2019 101 to No. 90 in 2020 amidst a backslide with his own hit tool projection as he tried to maximize his power. The Mets surprisingly broke camp with him, and even more surprisingly he stuck the entire season, playing his way up from fifth infielder to quasi-regular shortstop by the end of the season. Giménez's hit tool projection looked better, although not quite all the way back to the plus he was flashing in 2018, and his defense was extremely slick all over the infield even though he'd barely played second and third before.

I decided to put Giménez ahead of Rosario for now. Giménez is a plus defensive shortstop and younger, and offensively they're probably pretty close on true talent. Because of Rosario's bat speed and latent hit tool projection, he almost certainly still has higher upside, but he's over 1500 plate appearances deep and his plate approach has, if anything, regressed.

We've projected David Peterson as a no. 4 starter basically since he was drafted. He came up in 2020 and posted a 4.62 DRA, which is pretty much in line with that. Because he has a true out pitch—a gnarly slider—and the changeup flashed, he could theoretically start missing more bats at some point. If that happens, or his command improves, he could slide in as more of a no. 3 starter. Since he's proven the profile can work in the majors as-is, he slots in between the tier of 101 candidate prospects and the next group down, which is a tick up from his prospect days last year, where he was behind Wolf.

Part 3: Featured Articles

Mets All-Time Top 10 Players

by Rob Mains

POSITION PLAYERS

JOHN STEARNS, C (1975–1984)
From 1977 to 1982, Stearns made four All-Star teams—the first Met to do so—while hitting .265/.345/.382, outstanding for a catcher at the time. In his best season, 1978, he hit .264/.354/.413 with 15 homers and 25 stolen bases. The Mets were truly wretched during those years; their 67-95 record in 1980 was the best during the span. Known for his toughness, he fought through a series of nagging injuries before suffering an elbow injury in 1982 that effectively ended his career—he played only eight games after his 30th birthday.

MIKE PIAZZA, C (1998–2005)
He was already 29 when the Mets acquired him in May 1998, and he immediately became the team's key power source, hitting .303/.375/.569 with 170 homers and 505 RBI in his first four-and-change seasons. Age and injuries slowed him down after that, but he holds the team franchise record for OPS (.915), and trails only David Wright and Darryl Strawberry (below) in OPS. His go-ahead home run in the Mets' first home game after 9/11 is one of the most famous hits in baseball history.

KEITH HERNANDEZ, 1B (1983–1989)
He came to the Mets via a one-sided trade with St. Louis in 1983, joining the team during Tom Seaver's last year with the club. It was a changing of the guard: The leader of the first great Mets club leaving, the leader of the next great Mets clubs arriving. The Mets were first or second in the division for the rest of Hernandez' tenure. He wasn't a slugging first baseman but he had outstanding on-base skills (.297 batting average, .387 on-base percentage, both first in franchise history for players with 2,500 plate appearances) and a superlative glove.

EDGARDO ALFONZO, 2B (1995-2002)

He made only one All-Star team, and never led the league in anything, but he was an across-the-board solid player. He could hit for average (.292 with the Mets), get on base (.367 on-base percentage, sixth in club history), hit a dozen or two homers and as many as 41 doubles per season, and was an excellent second baseman. He had his best years in 1999 and 2000, helping the Mets win back-to-back division titles while hitting .313/.404/.520, scoring 232 runs, driving in 202, with 81 doubles and 52 homers. Back injuries robbed him of his second act.

HOWARD JOHNSON, 3B (1985-1993)

He was odd in some ways: HoJo was a switch-hitter who often struggled against lefties, an error-prone third baseman, a fast runner who looked lost in the outfield, and an impact hitter who slumped in even-numbered years. And yet, he was also good: Johnson, Wright, and Strawberry are the only players in team history with more than 100 homers and 100 stolen bases. Those are the only Mets to have 30 homers and 30 swipes in the same season, but Johnson did it three times: 1987, 1989, and 1991. Johnson's 192 homers and 202 stolen bases each rank third for the franchise. He had an .801 OPS in nine seasons with the club.

DAVID WRIGHT, 3B (2004-2016, 2018)

This list contains a lot of heartbreak, but if you're a Mets fan you anticipated that. Back problems, of course, cut the captain's career short, but what a career. He was an above-average hitter every year (other than his two-game cameo in 2018), hitting .296/.376/.491. Adjusted for his era, his .867 OPS was 33 percent above average. He hit 20 or ore homers six times, drove in 100 runs five times, stole 15 or more bases eight times, and won two Gold Gloves. He could do It all.

JOSE REYES, SS (2003-2011, 2016-2018)

His last three years with the club were bad and stained by his 2016 suspension for domestic violence (the Mets reacquired him after that), but he was a star during his first stint, with a live bat (.292 average), power for a middle infielder (.441 slugging percentage), and best base-stealing skills in club history (370 stolen bases, 80 percent success rate). From 2005 to 2008 he missed only 15 games and led the league in plate appearances, hits, and stolen bases. He holds the team record for steals in a season (78) and career (408).

MOOKIE WILSON, OF (1980-1989)

Known best for hitting the ground ball that rolled under Bill Buckner's legs in Game 6 of the 1986 World Series, Wilson became the Mets' regular centerfielder in 1981 and was with the club though 97-loss and 108-win seasons. He played a decent center field and was the first Met to steal more than 45 bases in a season, swiping 58, 54, and 46 in 1982-84. Generally impatient at the plate, he had to keep up his batting average and power production to be an offensive plus, and during his 1984-1988 peak he did just that, averaging .286/.335/.428, solid numbers for the period. A fan favorite, he ranks sixth in club history with 592 runs scored.

DARRYL STRAWBERRY, OF (1983–1990)
Strawberry was the National League Rookie of the Year in 1983 and an All-Star in every following year with the Mets. The first-overall pick of the 1980 draft, his career was overshadowed by addiction struggles that began when he was with the club, but he was a well-above-average hitter every year. During his Mets years he led the league in homers, was third in RBI, fifth in runs, second in slugging, and fifth in OPS. His 252 homers are the most in Mets history and his .878 OPS, adjusted for the seasons in which he played, is easily the best.

CARLOS BELTRÁN, OF (2005–2011)
Beltrán was one of the best players ever for two franchises, the Royals and the Mets, yet it's his lot to be remembered for his role in the Houston sign-stealing scandal and the called strike three he took to end the 2004 NLCS. Injuries limited him to just four full seasons in Flushing, during which he averaged 105 runs, 29 homers, 104 RBI, 21 stolen bases, an OPS 25 percent better than league average, and Gold Glove-quality defense.

PITCHERS

TOM SEAVER, RHP (1967–1977, 1983)
The Mets team pitching leader in just about everything—innings, starts, wins, strikeouts, complete games, shutouts—by a wide margin. His 2.57 ERA is the lowest as well. He won three Cy Young Awards with the Mets, pitching at least 236 innings every year with the club. His "midnight massacre" trade to the Reds and his end-of-life struggles with Lyme disease and dementia were a sad end to the man they called The Franchise, the finest player in team history.

JERRY KOOSMAN, LHP (1967–1978)
In his rookie season, Koosman went 19-12 with a 2.08 ERA in 263.2 innings and was top-10 in the league in starts, complete games, shutouts, strikeouts, ERA and wins, yet didn't win the Rookie of the Year award. That's what happens when you break in the same year as Johnny Bench. He was the team's no. 2 starter behind Seaver, sixth in the National League in innings and wins and fifth in strikeouts and ERA from 1968 to 1976. He and Seaver are the only Mets pitchers with over 2,500 innings pitched and his 3.09 Mets ERA is the fourth-lowest. Won 21 games in 1976, then lost 20 the next year, less due to poor pitching than to non-existent run support: The Mets gave him 3.3 runs per game in a league that averaged 4.4. After a second year like that the Mets traded him to his home-state Twins in a deal that brought back a young Jesse Orosco.

JON MATLACK, LHP (1971–1977)

The fourth-overall pick of the 1967 draft, Matlack was an excellent pitcher who toiled in the shadow of Seaver and Koosman. From his Rookie of the Year season in 1972 to the last of his three All-Star years as a Met in 1976, he had a 2.84 ERA and averaged 15 wins and 248 innings per year. Among NL starters, he was fourth in strikeouts and ERA and fifth in innings and starts during those years. Like many Mets, he was traded (for nothing of value) during the late-1970s teardown that coincided with the arrival of free agency.

RON DARLING, RHP (1983–1991)

He started at least 32 games and pitched at least 200 innings every year from 1984 to 1989, posting an 86-52 record and 3.40 ERA for a succession of good Mets teams. He was never the best pitcher in the rotation, outshone by Gooden and, later, Cone at the top of the rotation, but he was reliable and durable, finishing in the top 10 in the league in strikeouts four straight years. He and Hernandez are two-thirds of the best TV booth in the game today.

SID FERNANDEZ, LHP (1984–1993)

Fernandez struck out 22 percent of the batters he faced as a Met, the most in team history to that point. His .204 batting average allowed is the lowest in team history and his .612 OPS allowed trails only Seaver and deGrom. He had a 3.14 ERA in 250 games started for the Mets, posting three full-season ERAs below 3.00, and is fifth in innings all-time for the club. An extreme fly-ball pitcher who would sometimes go whole games without allowing a groundball, allowing the Mets to get an extra bat into the lineup by moving Howard Johnson to shortstop on the assumption he'd never see a chance.

DWIGHT GOODEN, RHP (1984–1994)

He pitched 191 innings (striking out 300) in A ball and 218, 286.2, and 250 in his first three years in the majors—at ages 18, 19, 20, and 21, respectively. That usage, as much or more than the drug and alcohol abuse that that led him to an unsuccessful drug rehab stint in 1987 and suspension for the entire 1995 season, resulted in a quick decline from a preposterous early peak (58-19, 2.28 his first three years, Cy Young Award with his 24-4, 1.53 ERA in 1985) to a just-good remaining eight years (3.52 ERA, 12-8 average record). It's difficult to imagine a present-day player ever becoming as big a sensation as young Doc was, with the side of a building in Midtown Manhattan covered in his image and it seeming as fitting as any other monumental structure on the landscape.

DAVID CONE, RHP (1987–1992, 2003)

Cone's trade to the Mets in 1987 is one of the best in team history (sorry, Ed Hearn). His 1,172 strikeouts are sixth in team history and his 3.13 ERA the seventh-lowest (minimum 700 innings) despite spending only four full seasons with the club. In his best year, 1988, he was 20-3 with a 2.22 ERA. He led the league in strikeouts in 1990 and 1991 and he whiffed 23 percent of the batters he faced, a proportion surpassed only by contemporary pitchers deGrom and Noah Syndergaard. Traded to the Blue Jays in August 1992 in return for Jeff Kent and Ryan Thompson, the former making for a second borderline Hall of Famer the Mets failed to retain.

RICK REED, RHP (1997–2001)
He was not initially popular on the team after joining the team as a free agent: Reed had been a replacement player during the 1994-95 work stoppage having crossed the line under threat of release by the Reds; he was supporting his uninsured diabetic mother. He was with the Mets only four and a half seasons, but he was the club's top starter in 1997 and 1998 and his .621 won-lost record (59-36) is second to Gooden's .649 in team history. A control artist, he walked only 4.4 percent of the batters he faced, the third-lowest proportion in the league, and had a 3.66 ERA as a Met.

AL LEITER, LHP (1998–2004)
He was 32 years old with 11 years in the majors when he joined the Mets via a trade from the Marlins. He immediately became the team's workhorse, throwing an average of 194 innings per year with the Mets, with a 3.42 ERA that was 24 percent better than the league average. His 94 wins rank sixth in franchise history. He won the Clemente Award for community service in 2000 and became a broadcaster upon retiring. It was quite the career for a prospect the Yankees overworked then ditched because he couldn't say healthy.

JACOB deGROM, RHP (2014–2020)
He was the 272nd player selected in the 2010 amateur draft and, to date, ranks ahead of almost all of the preceding 271. (Bryce Harper, Manny Machado, Chris Sale, Christian Yelich, and Andrelton Simmons might demur.) He's already fifth on the franchise strikeout list and has whiffed 29 percent of opponents, the most in team history. His ERA 2.61 ERA is 50 percent better than league average and his trophy case contains the 2014 Rookie of the Year and the 2018 and 2019 Cy Young Awards. Assuming three more years of excellence he'll make an interesting test of Hall of Fame voters' willingness to ignore the cheap drug that is pitcher won-lost records.

A Taxonomy of 2020 Abnormalities

by Rob Mains

I'm going to start this with a trivia question. Trust me, it's relevant. Don't bother skipping to the end of the article to find the answer, it's not there.

Only five players have appeared in 140 or more games for 16 straight seasons. Who are they?

It's a trivia question starting off an essay, so you know how this works: Whatever you guessed, you're wrong. It's okay. As someone who purchased this book, chances are good that you're an educated baseball fan. But the circumstances behind 2020 force us to abandon, or at least seriously question, some of our favorite patterns and crutches for evaluating the game we love.

We just completed what was undoubtedly the strangest season in MLB history. No fans, geographically limited schedule, universal DH, seven-inning twin bills, runners on second in extra innings, a 16-team postseason, a club playing at a Triple-A stadium. Some of these changes will likely persist (sorry), but we've never had so many tweaks dumped on us all at once, at least not since they figured out how many balls were in a walk.

And the biggest, of course, was the 60-game season. The 19th century was dotted with teams that went bankrupt before the season ended, but the lone season with only 60 scheduled games was 1877. That year there were only six teams, the league rostered a total of 77 players (just 16 more than the 2020 Marlins), and batters called for pitches to be thrown high or low by the pitcher, who was 50 feet away. We can say the 2020 season was easily the shortest ever for recognizable baseball.

As such, it'll stand out. Few abbreviated seasons do. Just about everybody reading this knows the 1994 season ended after Seattle's Randy Johnson struck out Oakland's Ernie Young for the last out of the Mariners-A's game on August 11. The ensuing player strike wiped out the rest of the season and the postseason. Teams played only 112-117 games that year.

And many of you know that a strike in the middle of the 1981 season split the season in two, resulting in the only Division Series until 1995. Teams played only 103-111 games that year, the shortest regular season since 1885.

Those two seasons are memorable. So when we see that nobody drove in 100 runs in 1981, or that Greg Maddux was the only pitcher with 180 or more innings pitched in 1994, we think, "Of course. Strike year."

But we don't remember other short years. You might not recall that the 1994 strike spilled into the next year, chopping 18 games off the 1995 schedule. You might've read that the 1918 season, played during the last pandemic, ended after Labor Day due to the government's World War I "work or fight" order. A strike erased the first week and a half of the 1972 season, but that year's best known as the last time pitchers batted in the American League.

The point is, while we don't remember small changes to the schedule, we remember the big ones. The 1981 mid-season strike. The 1994 season- and Series-ending strike. And, of course, the pandemic-shortened 2020 season. We won't need a reminder why Marcell Ozuna's 18 homers were the fewest to lead the National League in a century. (Literally; Cy Williams led with 15 in 1920.)

Now, about that trivia question. The five players are Hank Aaron, Brooks Robinson, Pete Rose, Ichiro Suzuki, and Johnny Damon. The one nobody gets, of course, is Damon, and a lot of people miss Ichiro, whose last season of 140-plus games came garbed in the red-orange and ocean blue of Miami when he was 42. That's half of what makes it a good question. The other half is the two guys whom many think made the list but didn't. Lou Gehrig? His streak started in the Yankees' 42nd game of the 1925 season and lasted only 13 seasons after that. And everybody assumes Cal Ripken Jr. did it, having played 2,632 straight games over 17 seasons. But one of those 17 seasons was 1994, when the Orioles played only 112 games.

My point? *I just told you* everybody remembers the 1994 strike year, but everybody forgets it fell in the middle of Ripken's streak, separating the first twelve years from the last four. Just because we recall something doesn't mean it's always at the front of our minds.

Nobody is going to forget 2020, and baseball is obviously not the main reason. But there will come a time in the future when you're looking at a player's or a team's record, and there will be baffling numbers there for 2020, and you'll think, "I wonder what happened." (Not to mention the missing line for minor league players.) Just like you forgot that the 1994 strike limited Ripken to 112 games.

Try not to forget it, though. The 2020 season resulted in weird statistical results for several reasons.

There were only 60 games.

I know, duh. But that had impacts beyond counting stats like Ozuna's home run total or Yu Darvish and Shane Bieber leading the majors with eight wins. (I know, pitcher wins, but still.)

The 162-game season is the longest among major North American sports, and that duration gives us a gift. Over the course of a long season, small variations tend to even out. A player who has a ten-game hot streak will probably have a ten-game cold streak. A team that starts the year losing a bunch of close games will probably win a bunch of them. We get regression to the mean. Statistics stabilize.

Consider flipping a coin. Over the long run, we expect it to come up heads about half the time. But the fewer flips, the more variation there'll be. If you flip a coin six times, probability theory tells us you'll get at least two-third heads about 34 percent of the time. Flip it 30 times, your chance of two-thirds heads drops to five percent.

Or, relevant to this case, if you flip a coin 60 times, your chance of getting at least 36 heads—that's 60 percent—is 7.75 percent. Expand the coin-flipping to 162 times, and the chance of getting 60 percent heads drops to 0.73 percent.

In other words, the odds of an outcome that's 20 percent better (or worse) than expected is *more than ten times higher* when you flip your coin 60 times than when you do it 162 times. Call it small sample size, call lack of mean reversion, or call it luck not evening out, 162 is a lot more predictive than 60. You get much more variation over 60 games than over 162. Bieber's 1.63 ERA and 0.87 FIP aren't something we'd see over a full season, and neither is Javier Baéz's .203/.238/.360.

Some players' lines in 2020 look normal. Brian Anderson had an .811 OPS in 2019 and an .810 OPS in 2020. (He probably would have gotten that last point if he'd been given enough time.) But there are many like Bieber and Baéz, some of them from young players still establishing their talent levels. The answer to the question, "What went right or wrong for that guy in 2020?" is most likely "Nothing, it was just a 2020 thing."

Preseason training was abbreviated for hitters.
Every year, spring training drags. Players get tired of it, fans get tired of it, and you sure can tell sportswriters get tired of it. Yes, something to get everyone into shape is necessary, but does it really have to drag on for over a month? Can't we shorten it?

The 2020 season answered in the negative, at least for hitters. Warren Spahn is credited with saying that hitting is timing and pitching is upsetting timing. It appears nobody had his timing down after the abbreviated July summer camp. Through August 9—18 games into the season—MLB batters were hitting .230/.311/.395 with a .275 BABIP. That BABIP, had it held, would have been the lowest since 1968, the Year of the Pitcher. In recent years it's hovered around .300.

It didn't hold. Play returned to more normal levels the rest of the year: .249/.325/.425 with a .297 BABIP starting August 10. But batters whose play concentrated in those first two weeks wound up with ugly lines. Andrew

Benintendi went on the injured list with a season-ending rib cage strain on August 11. His final line: .103/.314/.128 in 14 games. Franchy Cordero went on the IL with a hamate bone fracture on August 9 and a .154/.185/.231 line. Even though he came back strong in a late September return, it was too late to repair his full-season numbers.

Preseason training was abbreviated for pitchers.
Every year, spring training drags. Players get tired of it, fans get tired of it … wait, I already said that. But the abbreviated preseason was tough on pitchers, too. As noted, they had the upper hand coming out of the gate. But then they lost that hand. And then their arms, too.

The 2020 season was spread over 67 days. During those 67 days, 237 pitchers hit the Injured List, compared to 135 in the first 67 days of 2019. A lot of those IL stints, though, were COVID-19-related. Still, over the first 67 days of the 2019 season, there were 72 pitchers on the IL with arm injuries. That figure jumped to 110 in 2020, a 53 percent increase.

There are a number of factors contributing to pitcher arm injuries, ranging from usage to velocity, but it appears that attenuated preseason training played a role. A lot of pitchers had super-short seasons due to arm woes. Corey Kluber, Roberto Osuna, and Shohei Ohtani combined for seven innings, none after August 8. All suffered arm injuries. We'll never know whether they'd have fared better with a longer preseason, but we can guess how they probably feel.

Everybody played.
Rosters were set to expand from 25 to 26 in 2020, so even if we'd had a normal season, we'd have likely seen 2019's record of 1,410 players on MLB rosters broken. But due to the pandemic, rosters started the year at 30 and were cut to only 28. Add multiple COVID-19 absences and the revolving door caused by poor starts by hitters and a rash of pitcher arm injuries, and 1,289 players appeared in MLB games in 2020. The comparable figure over the first 67 days of the 2019 season was 1,109. That 16 percent increase works out to an average of six more players per team in 2020 compared to a similar slice of 2019. A future look back at 2020 rosters will include a lot of unfamiliar names.

Plus became a minus.
In advanced metrics, we adjust batter and pitcher performance for park and league/era variations. A plus sign appended to the end of a measure means that it's adjusted for park and league. It's scaled to an average of 100, with higher figures above average and lower figures below average. (Similarly, a metric with a minus is also park- and league-adjusted and scaled to 100, with lower values better.) Here at BP, our advanced measure of offensive performance is DRC+. Baseball-Reference has OPS+ and FanGraphs has wRC+.

Using park and league adjustments, we can compare Dante Bichette's 1995 Steroid Era season at pre-humidor Coors Field (.340/.364/.620, 40 homers, 128 RBI, MVP runner-up) with Jim Wynn's 1968 Year of the Pitcher season at the cavernous Astrodome (.269/.376/.474, 26 homers, 67 RBI, no MVP votes). It's not close. DRC+, OPS+, and wRC+ all give the nod to Wynn, handily. This is a useful tool. As my Baseball Prospectus colleague Patrick Dubuque tweeted last fall, "Please note that when I ask how you are, I am already adjusting for era."

The 2020 season messes up plus (and minus) stats for two reasons. First, the park adjustment was based on only 30 home games instead of the usual 81. Everything noted above regarding the short season applies, literally doubly, to park effect calculations. DRC+ uses a single-season park factor. OPS+ uses a three-year average and wRC+ five years. The figure for 2020 is suspect.

Second, OPS+ and wRC+ adjust for league: American and National. (DRC+ adjusts for opponent, regardless of league.) While there were two leagues in 2020, they were an artificial construct. To reduce travel, teams played opponents geographically, not based on league. There weren't two leagues, American and National. There were three, Western, Central, and Eastern.

That makes a difference because teams in the same league played in different run-scoring environments. AL teams scored 4.58 runs per game, NL teams 4.71. That's a small difference. But teams in the East scored 0.21 more runs per game (4.95) than teams in the West (4.74), and they both scored a lot more than Central teams (4.25). Adjusting for league misses that difference, so this book will be safe in that regard, but other sources may be distorted somewhat.

Not every game was a "game."

In 2020, the rising tide of strikeouts was finally stemmed. Strikeouts per team per game fell from 8.8 in 2019 to 8.7 in 2020. That marked the first decline after 14 straight annual increases.

In 2020, the rising tide of strikeouts rose higher. Batters struck out in 23.4 percent of plate appearances compared to 23.0 percent in 2019. That marked the 15th straight annual increase.

Both are true statements.

Because of two rule changes—seven-inning doubleheaders and runners on second in extra innings—games in 2020 were unprecedented in their brevity. There were 37.0 plate appearances per game in 2020. The only years with fewer were 1904 and 1906-1909. The average game in 2020 entailed 8.61 innings pitched, the fewest since 1899.

So when you see any per-game stats for 2020, you need to increase them by 3 or 4 percent to get them on equal footing with recent years.

Or, better, just ignore them. Last year happened. There were major league games contested between major league teams. But when you're looking at those physical or electronic baseball cards, when you're weaving narratives over why this young player's inevitable rise to stardom fell apart or why that old veteran rekindled his magic, don't linger on the 2020 line. It was just too weird.

Thanks to Lucas Apostoleris for research assistance.

—*Rob Mains is an author of Baseball Prospectus.*

Tranches of WAR

by Russell A. Carleton

We ask "replacement level" to be a lot of things. Sometimes contradictory things. Sometimes I wonder if we know what it even means anymore. The original idea was that it represented the level of production that a team could expect to get from "freely available talent", including bench players, minor leaguers, and waiver wire pickups. It created a common benchmark to compare everyone to, and for that reason, it represented an advancement well beyond what was available at the time. In fact, it created a language and a framework for evaluating players that was not just better but *entirely* different than what came before it.

But then we started mumbling in that language. The idea behind "wins above replacement" was one part sci-fi episode and one part mathematical exercise. Imagine that a player had disappeared before the season and suddenly, in an alternate timeline, his team would have had to replace him. The distance between him and that replacement line was his value. We need to talk about that alternate timeline.

Without getting too into 2:00 am "deep conversations" with extensive navel-gazing, it's worth thinking about why one player might not be playing, while another might.

- A player might not be playing because he has a short-term injury or his manager believes that he needs a day off.
- A player might not be playing because he has a longer-term injury that requires him to be on the injured list.

There's a difference here between these two situations. In particular, the first one generally *doesn't* involve a compensatory roster move, while the second one does. It's possible, though not guaranteed, that the person who will be replacing the injured/resting player would be the same in either case. That matters. Teams generally carry a spare part for all eight position players on the diamond, although in the era of a four-player bench, those spare parts usually are the backup plan for more than one spot.

New York Mets 2021

A couple of years ago, I posed a hypothetical question. Suppose that a team had two players in its system fighting for a fourth outfielder spot. One of them was a league average hitter, but would be worth 20 runs below average if allowed to play center field for a full season. One of them was a perfectly average fielder, but would be 15 runs below average as a hitter, if allowed to play an entire season. Which of the two should the team roster? It's tempting to say the second one, as overall, he is the better player. That misses the point. A league average hitter on the bench isn't just a potential replacement for an injured outfielder. He might also pinch hit for the light-hitting shortstop in a key spot. You keep the average hitter on the roster, even though he isn't a hand-in-glove fit for one specific place on the field, because being a bench player is a different job description than being a long-term fill-in for someone. If you find yourself in need of a longer-term fill-in, you can bring the other guy up from AAA.

When we're determining the value of an everyday player though, if he had disappeared before the season and a team would have had to replace his production, they likely would have done it with a player who was a long-term fill-in type because they would have had to replace a guy who played everyday. Maybe that's the same guy that they would have rostered on their bench anyway, but we don't know. It gets to the query of what we hope to accomplish with WAR. Are we looking for an accurate modeling of reality or are we looking for a common baseline to compare everyone to? Both have their uses, but they are somewhat different questions.

Let's talk about another dichotomy.

- A player might not be playing because he isn't very good and is a bench-level player.
- A player might not be playing because there is another player on the team who has a situational advantage that makes him the better choice today. The classic case of this is a handedness platoon. On another day, he might be a better choice.

When we think about player usage, I think we're still stuck in the model that there are starters and there are scrubs. We have plenty of words for bench players or reserves or backups or utility guys. We do still have the word "platoon" in our collective vocabulary, but in the age of short benches, it's hard to construct one. It's always been hard to construct them. You have to find two players who hit with different hands, have skill sets that complement each other, and probably play the same position. In the era of the short bench, one of them had probably better double as a utility player in some way. Baseball has a two-tiered language geared toward the idea of regulars and reserves. The fact that it was so easy for me to find plenty of synonyms for "a player whose primary function is to come into a game to replace a regular player if he is injured or resting" should tell you something.

I'm always one to look for "unspoken words" in baseball. What is it called when someone is both half of a platoon and the utility infielder? That guy exists sometimes, but he reveals himself in that role—usually by accident. We don't have a word for that, and whenever I find myself saying "we don't have a word for that", I look for new opportunities. What do you call it, further, when the job of being the utility infielder is decentralized across the whole infield with occasional contributions from the left fielder? It's not even a "super-utility" player. What happens when you build your entire roster around the idea that everyone will be expected to be a triple major?

⚾   ⚾   ⚾

I think someone else beat me to this one, and on a grand scale. Platoons work because we know that hitters of the opposite hand to the pitcher get better results than hitters of the same hand, usually to the tune of about 20 points of OBP. If you want to express that in runs, it usually comes out to somewhere around 10 to 12 runs of linear weights value prorated across 650 PA. But hang on a second, now let's say that we have two players who might start today, both of roughly equal merit with the bat. One has a handedness advantage, but is the worse fielder of the two. In that case, as long as his "over the course of a season" projection as a fielder at whatever position you want to slot him into is less than a 10-run drop from the guy he might replace, then he's a better option today.

We're not used to thinking of utility players as bat-first options, who would play below-average defense at three different infield positions. That guy might hook on as a 2B/3B/LF type (Howie Kendrick, come on down!) but teams usually think to themselves that they need as their utility infielder someone who "can handle" shortstop, the toughest of the infield spots to play. If someone can do that *and* hit well, he's probably already starting somewhere, so he's not available as a utility infielder. It's easier for those glove guys to find a job. In a world where the replacement for a shortstop *has to be* the designated utility infielder, that makes sense.

But as we talked about last week, we're living in a different world. The rate at which a replacement for a regular starter turns out to be *another starter* shifting over to cover has gone way up over the last five years. There was always some of it in the game, but this has been a supernova of switcheroos. Now if your second baseman is capable of playing a decent shortstop, that 2B/3B/LF guy can swap in. He's not actually playing shortstop, and maybe the defense suffers from the switch, but if he's got enough of a bat, he might outhit those extra fielding miscues. And in doing so, he is effectively your backup shortstop.

Somewhere along the lines, teams got hip to the idea of multi-positional play from their regulars. I've written before about how you can't just put a player, however athletic, into a new position and expect much at first. The data tell us that. Eventually, players can learn to be multi-positionalists, but it takes time, roughly on the order of two months, before they're OK. But there's a hidden message in there. If you give a player some reps at a new spot, he's a reasonably gifted athlete and somewhat smart and willing to learn, he could probably pick it up enough to get to "good enough," and it doesn't take forever. You just have to be purposeful about it. Maybe you get to the point where you can start to say "he's still below average but we could move him there and get another bat into the lineup, and it's a net win."

Teams have started to build those extra lessons into their player development program. It used to be seen as a mark of weakness to be relegated to "utility player" because that meant that you were a bench player (all those synonyms above come with a side of stigma). Now, it's a way of building a team. If you get a few reps in the minors (where it doesn't count) at a spot, you'll have at least played the spot at game speed before. There are limits to how far you can push that. A slow-footed "he's out in left field because we don't have the DH" guy is never going to play short, but maybe your third baseman can try second base and not look like a total moose out there.

⚾ ⚾ ⚾

Back to WAR. I'd argue that the world of starters and scrubs is slowly disintegrating, for good cause. In the event that a regular starter really does go down with an injury–ostensibly, the alternate universe scenario that WAR is attempting to model–it makes the team a little more resilient to replacing him. And the good news is that you're more likely to be able to replace him with the best of the bench bunch, rather than the third-best guy, because the best guy doesn't have to be an exact positional match for the guy who got hurt. And that's what the manager would want to do. He'd want to replace that long-term production, not with an amalgam of everyone else who played that position, but with the best guy available from his reserves.

Now this is still WAR. We still want to retain the principle that we should be measuring a player, and not his teammates. We need some sort of common baseline, and despite what I just said, we'll still need some sort of amalgam. To construct that, I give to you the idea of the tranche. The word, if you've not heard it before, refers to a piece of a whole that is somehow segmented off. It's often used in finance to talk about layers of a financial instrument.

Here, I want you to consider that there are 30 starters at each of the seven non-battery positions (catchers should have their own WAR, since only a catcher can replace a catcher). We can identify them by playing time, and we can futz around with the definition a little bit if we need to. Next, among those who aren't in that starting pool, we identify the top tranche of the 30 best bench players, which I would again identify by playing time, and then the second and third and fourth and so on. If a player were to disappear, his manager would probably want to take a guy from that top tranche of the bench to replace him. In a world where even the starters can slide around the field, that becomes more feasible.

We can take a look at that top tranche and say "How many of them showed that they are able to play (first, second, etc.)?" and therefore could have directly substituted for the starter? How many of them could have been a direct substitute for our injured player? We don't know whether one of them would be on *a specific* team, but we can say that 40 percent of the time, a manager would have been able to draw from tranche 1 in filling the role, and 35 percent from tranche 2. But on tranche 1, we can also look at how many of those players played a position that could have then shifted and covered for that spot. We'd need some eligibility criteria for all of this (probably a minimum number of games played) but it would just be a matter of multiplication. Shortstop would be harder to fill, and managers would probably be dipping a little further down in the talent pool, and so replacement level would be lower, as it is now.

Doing some quick analysis, I found that the difference in just batting linear weights (haven't even gotten into running or fielding) between tranche 1 and tranche 2 in 2019 was about 6.5 runs, prorated across 650 PA. Between tranche 1 and tranche 3, it's 10.8 runs. The ability to shift those plate appearances up the ladder has some real value.

This part is important. We can also give credit to starters for the positions that they showed an ability to play, even if they didn't play them (this is the guy fully capable of playing center, but who's in a corner because the team already has a good center fielder) because he allows a team to carry a player who hits like a left fielder to functionally be the team's backup center fielder. He facilitates that movement upward among the tranches. We can start to appreciate the difference between a left fielder who would never be able to hack it in center (and the compensatory move that his team would have to make) and the left fielder who could do it, but just didn't have to very often.

Past that, you can continue to use whatever hitting and fielding and running metrics you like to determine a player's value, but when we get down to constructing that baseline, I'd argue we need a better conceptual and mathematical framework. It's going to require some more #GoryMath than we're used to, but I'd argue it's a better conceptualization of the way that MLB actually plays the game in 2020. If...y'know...MLB plays in 2020. If WAR is going to be our flagship statistic among the *acronymati*, then we need to acknowledge that it contains some old and starting-to-be-out-of-date assumptions about the game. We may need to tinker with it. Here's my idea for how.

—*Russell A. Carleton is an author of Baseball Prospectus.*

Secondhand Sport

by Patrick Dubuque

Back before time stopped, I liked to go to thrift stores. Now that I'm older, I rarely ever buy anything—I don't need much in my life, now—but I still enjoy the old familiar circuit: check to see if there are baseball cards to write about, look for board or card games to play with the kids, scan for random ironic jerseys, hit the book section. It takes ten, maybe fifteen minutes. Thrift stores are the antithesis of modern online shopping, because you don't know what they have, and you don't even really know what you want. It's junk, literal junk, stuff other people thought was worthless. That's what makes it great.

In an idealized economy, thrift stores shouldn't exist. Everybody has a living wage, and every product has a durability that exactly matches its desired life; nothing should need to be given away, no one should need to be given to. But then, thrift stores shouldn't work on a customer experience level, either. You wouldn't think an ethos of "let's make everything disorganized and hard to find" would lead to customer satisfaction, but low-budget retailers like TJ Maxx and Ross thrive on this model. People like bargain hunting as much for the hunting as the bargain; it's part of the experience, spending time as if it's a wager. There's a thrill, occasionally, in inefficiency.

In sports, the modern overuse of the word "inefficiency" is a condemnation: It insinuates that there is *an* efficiency, a correct way to be found, and that all other ways are wrong ways. It's prevalent in baseball but hardly contained to it; the lifehack, the Silicon Valley disruption are other examples of productivity creep in our daily lives. Their modern success makes plenty of sense. Maximization of resources, after all, is its own puzzle, and an industry of European board games is founded upon it. It's fun to take a system and optimize it, unravel it like a sudoku puzzle. If there's only one kind of genius, after all, there's no way anyone can fail to appreciate it.

Baseball has been hacking away at these perceived inefficiencies since its inception: platoons, bullpens, farm systems were all installed to extract more out of the tools at hand. But it's been a particular badge of the sabermetric movement, from Ken Phelps and his All-Star Team to Ricardo Rincon and the darlings of *Moneyball*. It's business, but it's also an ethos: the idea that there's treasure among the trash, something we all failed to appreciate until someone brought it to light.

It's the myth that made Sidd Finch so enticing, that fuels so many "best shape" narratives and new pitch promises. We all, athletes and unathletic sportswriters, want to believe that there's genius trapped inside us, and that it's just a matter of puzzling out the combination to unlock it. That our art, our style is the next inefficiency, waiting for our own Billy Beane. It's why we root for underdogs, and why we're excited for the Mike Tauchmans and the Eurubiel Durazos, champions of skin-deep mediocrity.

Except we aren't anymore, really. The days of "Free X" have descended beyond the ring of irony and into obscurity. There are still Xs to be freed, or at least one X, duplicated endlessly: Mike Ford, Luke Voit, Max Muncy. The undervalued one-dimensional slugger demonstrated how the game hasn't quite culturally caught up to its logical extreme. But for those who don't fit the rather spacious mold, times are grimmer. As Rob Arthur revealed several months ago, there's been a marked increase in the number of sub-replacement relievers. It's the outcome of a greater number of teams forced to play out games without the talent to win them, but it's also emblematic of the modern tendency of teams to dispose of their disposable assets, burning through cost-controlled arms the way that man chopped down forests in *The Lorax*. Stuff just isn't built to outlive their original owners anymore.

It's unsurprising, given how well-mined the market for inefficiencies has been of late. The disciples of the early analytics departments, and the disciples of those, have proliferated the league, with only a few backwater holdouts. The league has grown smarter, but every team has learned the same lesson. In fact, the phenomenon creates a peculiar kind of feedback loop: As teams value a specific subset of players or skills, prospective athletes learn to increase their own marketability by conforming themselves to the demands of their prospective employers.

And that's tragic, in the way that the extinction of animals is tragic; a certain amount of biodiversity in baseball has been lost. Shortstops hit like outfielders. Pitchers don't hit at all. Only the catchers remain idiosyncratic, thanks to the defensive demands of their position; eventually they too will be required to produce like everyone else, or they'll meet the fate of their battery mates. A perfect economy requires perfect production.

I mentioned earlier that more and more, I leave thrift stores empty-handed. It is true that I am more discerning than in the past; my bookshelves are full, and there are more streaming films than I will ever be able to watch. But there are other factors at play.

Thrift stores are, in a way, the bond markets of retail. When the economy is rough and other retailers are struggling, more people look secondhand for their products. But as recently as last year, publications were noting a reversal of the trend: Companies like Goodwill and Savers were expanding despite a strong economy. Publications credited a heightened sense of environmentalism and a rejection of cutting-edge fashion as drivers behind the increase, though the more likely answer is the modern American economy hasn't showered its favors equally, particularly among the young.

But it is more than just the economy. Baseball and thrift stores share something else in common, evident in our current conversations about restarting the sport: They live in the gray area between public service and private enterprise. Thrift stores provide affordable necessities to lower-class citizens, and collectibles and fashion for the middle-class. Because of the success of the latter, prices have gone up across the board. Especially in terms of clothing, the middle-class flight from fashion into vintage has instead carried the aftereffects of fashion, including its costs, into a territory where people just want clothes. But there's another factor in the rise of prices, in the form of the internet.

The Goodwills of the world have grown smarter, too, employing the internet to extract full value from their detritus. Ebay, similarly, has lost much of the charm it had as a new frontier around the turn of the century. Everything has a price point now; even individual taste is no match for the algorithm, because anything rare, no matter how niche its market, is a collectible to someone.

The internet has had the same effect on thrift stores that sabermetrics has had on baseball; its equivalent to OBP was the bar scanner. As detailed in Slate, the rise of second-party stores on eBay and Amazon birthed an entire industry of used-good salespeople, armed with PDAs and scanners, buying books for three dollars to sell online for five. The author, Michael Savitz, reports earning $60,000 by working nearly 80 hours a week; he makes it clear that this is not a vocation of his choosing. It's long hours, with no real creativity or individuality, skimming the cream off of a local establishment and flipping it to someone with a little more money on the other side of the country. And once the vocation exists, the obvious question arises: why wait to put the wares out on the shelves? Why allow value to exist at all?

Nothing is ruined. Thrift stores will continue to sell polo shirts and DVDs, and baseball will continue to exist and make or lose money, depending on who you believe. But as we continue to refine our knowledge, we lose something in the conquest for efficiency, a delight born out of the unknown. The problem isn't the efficiency itself; we can't blame the booksellers, or the people sweeping freeways to collect grams of platinum from damaged catalytic converters. The problem is a system that requires this sort of profit-skimming behavior in order to feed families (or, for corporations, maximize shareholder return).

In times like these, with the 2020 season on the brink and the collective bargaining agreement close behind, it can often feel like the current situation is untenable. It can't keep going like this, even if we don't know what to do about it. But as with thrift stores, there's an equally irresistible feeling that it *has* to keep going, that it would be unimaginable to not have this broken, amazing sport. Both industries exist on an invisible foundation of friction, of chaos and unpredictability, even as both see their foundations buffed down to a perfect, untouchable polish. But if COVID-19 and its financial ramifications do, as some have suggested, make it such that the baseball that returns is fundamentally different than the baseball that came before, perhaps this is the time to lean in, and change the game even more. Fix bunting. Make defense more difficult. Create viable, alternate strategies. Add some chaos back into baseball. It's fun when no one knows quite where things are.

—Patrick Dubuque is an author of Baseball Prospectus.

Steve Dalkowski Dreaming

by Steven Goldman

We dream of being a pitcher, of starring in the major leagues. Depending on your age and your sense of historical perspective, you might imagine yourself as Walter Johnson, throwing harder than anyone else—hitting more batters than anyone else, too, but always feeling bad about it. You could picture yourself as a Tom Seaver or a David Cone, with all the stuff in the world but still being cerebral about it, thinking about so much more than burning 'em in there. There are so many models one could choose: You could be a Lefty Gomez, Jim Bouton, or Bill Lee, skilled, but not taking the whole thing too seriously, or a Lefty Grove, Bob Gibson, or Steve Carlton, powerful but treating each start like a mission to be survived instead of a game to be enjoyed.

Very few would dream of being Steve Dalkowski, the former Baltimore Orioles prospect who died of COVID-19 last week at the age of 80. Yet, there is something just as noble in Dalkowski's negative accomplishments—and accomplishments is what they are—as there is in the precision-engineered pitching of a Greg Maddux. You have to be very good to be that bad. Dalkowski had all of the stuff of the greatest pitchers but none of the command; his story is not one of failing to conquer his limitations, but striving against one of the cruelest hands that fate or genetics or personality can deal us: A desire to achieve great things which is almost but not quite matched by the ability to meet that goal.

As with Johnson, Grove, Bob Feller, and the rest of the hard-throwing pitchers who played before the advent of modern radar guns, we have to take the word of the players and coaches who saw Dalkowski pitch as to his velocity. He was a hard-drinking, maximum-effort pitcher who, if their memories are to be believed, consistently threw over 100 miles per hour. His was the Maltese Fastball, the stuff that dreams are made of. The problem is that velocity without command and control is still a good distance from utility. Dalkowski was the most effective towel you could design for a fish, the sleekest bathing suit intended to be worn by an astronaut, but that doesn't mean he wasn't beautiful: We can appreciate a journey even if it doesn't end at the intended destination.

Whether because of sloppy mechanics he couldn't calm, an inability to understand that a consistent 98 in the strike zone would likely be more effective than a consistent 110 out of it, or all that beer, Dalkowski could never make the adjustments that pitchers like Feller and Nolan Ryan made before him, possibly because he had so far to go: Feller, who never pitched in the minors, came up at 17 and spent three years walking almost seven batters per nine innings before settling in at 3.8 beginning when he was 20. Ryan started out walking over six batters per nine but gradually improved as his long career played out; for him to go from 6.2 walks per nine with the 1966 Greenville Mets to 3.7 with the 1989 Texas Rangers represents a 40 percent reduction. An equivalent improvement by Dalkowski would still have left him walking over 11 batters per nine innings.

Dalkowski was like *The Room* of pitchers, a player so bad he became good again. Cal Ripken, Sr., who both played with and managed Dalkowski, recalled in a 1979 *Sporting News* "where are they now" piece the occasion when the pitcher crossed up his catcher and his fastball, "hit the plate umpire smack in the mask. The mask broke all to pieces and the umpire wound up in the hospital for three days with a concussion. If they ever had a radar gun in those days, I'll bet Dalkowski would have been timed at 110 miles an hour."

Signed by the Orioles out of New Britain High in Connecticut in 1957, Dalkowski was sent to Kingsport in the Appalachian League, where he pitched 62 innings. He allowed only 22 hits in 62 innings, or 3.2 per nine, a number with no equivalent in major league history (though Aroldis Chapman came close in 2014), and also struck out 121 (17.6 per nine) and walked 129 (18.7). He was also charged with 39 wild pitches. That June, one of his fastballs clipped a Dodgers prospect named Bob Beavers and carried away part of his ear. "The first pitch was over the backstop, the second pitch was called a strike, I didn't think it was," Beavers said last year. "The third pitch hit me and knocked me out, so I don't remember much after that. I couldn't get in the sun for a while, and I never did play baseball again." Former minor leaguer Ron Shelton based the *Bull Durham* pitcher Nuke LaLoosh on Dalkowski. And yet, to see him as a figure of fun, an amusing loser, is to misunderstand something unique and strange.

Dalkowski kept on posting some of the strangest lines in baseball history. Pitching for the Stockton Ports of the Class C California League in 1960, he struck out 262 and walked 262 in 170 innings. Yet, he did improve, especially after pitching for Earl Weaver at Elmira in 1962. Weaver had previously had Dalkowski at Aberdeen in 1959, but wasn't ready to grapple with him then. This time he was. "I had grown more and more concerned about players with great physical abilities who could not learn to correct certain basic deficiencies no matter how much you instructed or drilled them," he related in his autobiography, *It's What You Learn After You Know It All That Counts*. He got permission from the Orioles to give all of his players the Stanford-Binet IQ test. "Dalkowski finished in the 1 percentile in his ability to understand facts. Steve, it was said to say, had the ability to do everything but learn." [sic]

IQ tests are problematic diagnostic tools, so take Weaver's estimate of Dalkowski's mental capabilities with a grain of salt. What's important is that even if he got to the right answer by way of the wrong reason, Weaver had learned something valuable. His insight was to stop asking Dalkowski to learn new pitches and just let him get by with the two that he had. Were Dalkowski a prospect today, that would have been a no-brainer: Can't develop a third pitch? The bullpen is right over there, sir. Player development wasn't like that then, but Weaver, temporarily Dalkowski's mentor, could let him work with what he had. According to Weaver, the pitcher responded: "In the final 57 innings he pitched that season Dalkowski gave up 1 earned run, struck out 110 batters, and walked only 11." It's not true—as per the *Elmira Star-Gazette*, as of late July, Dalkowski had walked 71 in 106 innings and finished with 114 in 160 innings, which means Dalkowski's control actually faded at the end of the season rather than improved—but that doesn't mean it didn't happen in some sense, just that it didn't happen that way. Again, it's the journey, not the destination, and his ERA was 3.04 so *something* had gone right.

Also along the way: The next spring, Orioles manager Billy Hitchcock was rooting for Dalkowski to make the team as a long-man—maybe Weaver had gotten through to him. There were things out of Weaver's control, like the universe's twisted sense of humor: that March, Dalkowski's elbow went "twang."

You sometimes read that it was the Orioles' insistence on Dalkowski learning the curve that did him in, but even if they hadn't learned their lesson, the injury was probably just a coincidence: Dalkowski had thrown an incredible number of pitches over the previous few years. Still, it testifies to the dangers of trying to get what you want and risking the loss of what you had. Dalkowski tried to come back, but the 110-mph stuff was gone. A pitcher with no control and no stuff is...a civilian. What followed were years of vagabond living, arrests for drunkenness. There were Alcoholics Anonymous meetings, assistance from baseball alumni associations, but none of it took. From the 1990s until the time of his passing he dwelt in an assisted living facility, suffering from alcohol-related dementia. He'd been a heavy drinker since his teenage years. As with all those pitches per game, there was a price to be paid. You make choices on the journey and some of them are irrevocable. It's like a fairy tale: "Bite of poison apple? Don't mind if I do."

In the aforementioned *Sporting News* profile, Chuck Stevens, the head of the Association of Professional Ballplayers of America, a ballplayer charity, said, "I've got nothing against drinking. I do it myself sometimes. But, I don't condone common drunkenness. We went through lots of heartache and many dollars, but Dalkowski didn't want to help himself and we weren't going to keep him drunk." The journey is *un*like a fairy tale: No one will come along and kiss it better, not if they're busy forming judgments.

In the end, we are left with a sort of philosophical chicken/egg conundrum: Is failing to meet your goals evidence of unfulfilled potential or the lack of it? Isn't what you did by definition what you were capable of doing? Or could you have broken through to something better with the right help, the right lucky break? These are unanswerable questions, and how we try to answer them may say more about us than about the people we're judging.

No pitcher ever has it easy. *All* pitchers must work hard. *All* pitchers must refine their craft. It's almost never just about *stuff*. Dalkowski dreaming is no insult to the great pitchers who made it; from Pete Alexander to Max Scherzer, they have all earned their way up. And yet, if it is true that we can only do as much as we can do, then the journey would be more of an adventure, the ultimate triumph or defeat more noble, if like Dalkowski we lacked 100 percent of the confidence, the command, the self-possession, the commitment, the resistance to making bad decisions that so many great players possess—to be gloriously human. Or, to put it more succinctly, it would be fun to be able to throw as hard as any person ever has. Even if just for a moment, and even if nothing more came of it than that, no one could say you hadn't lived life to the fullest.

—*Steven Goldman is an author of Baseball Prospectus.*

A Reward For A Functioning Society

by Cory Frontin and Craig Goldstein

On July 5, Nationals reliever Sean Doolittle said in the middle of a press conference regarding the restart of Major League Baseball and what would later be known as summer camp, "sports are like the reward of a functioning society." This sentence was amidst a much longer, thoughtful reply about the societal and health conditions under which MLB players were being brought back. It's a very similar sentiment to one Jane McManus used on April 7, when she discussed the White House's meeting with sports commissioners. She said "sports are the effect of a functioning society—not the precursor."

Both versions of the same sentiment spoke to a laudable ideal in the context of a country that was not addressing a rampaging virus, and opting instead to bring sports back for the feeling of normalcy rather than the reality of it. "Priorities," as McManus said.

On Wednesday, the NBA's Milwaukee Bucks conducted a wildcat/political strike, refusing to come out for Game 5 of their playoff series against the Orlando Magic. The Magic refused to accept the forfeit, and shortly thereafter other playoff series were threatened by player strikes. Eventually the league moved to postpone that day's games, folding to players leveraging their united power.

The backdrop against which these actions took place was the shooting by police of Jacob Blake. Blake was shot in the back seven times by police, as he attempted to get into his vehicle. He managed to survive the assault, but is paralyzed from the waist down.

⚾ ⚾ ⚾

The step taken to walk out, first by the Milwaukee Bucks, then subsequently by other NBA, WNBA, and MLB teams, was a step toward upholding the virtue of the sentiment described by McManus and Doolittle. But that sentiment does not align with the broad history of sports in this and other countries, a history that contradicts the core of the idealistic statement.

Sports have been a significant part of American society for most of its existence, expanding in importance and influence in recent years. The idea that society was functioning in a way that was worthy of the reward of sports for most of that time is laughable. Much of America is not functioning and has not functioned for Black people, full stop. The oppressed people at the center of this political act by players, specifically Black players, in concert throughout the NBA and in fits and starts throughout Major League Baseball, have not known a society that functions for them rather than *because* of them.

Politics has been part of the sports landscape since the inception of sport, but for just about as long people have bemoaned its presence. Sports are to be an escape, it is said. An escape from what, though? A functioning society?

No, the presence of sports has never signified a cultural or political system that is on the up and up. Rather, the presence of sports *reflect and reinforce the society that produces them.*

⚾   ⚾   ⚾

The Negro Leagues were born out of societal dysfunction. The need for entirely separate leagues, composed of Black and Latino players barred from the Major Leagues because of racism? That is not a functioning society, and yet there were sports.

Even the integration of players from the Negro Leagues resulted in a transfer of power and wealth from Black-owned businesses and communities and into white ones, mirroring the dysfunction that had bled into every aspect of American society at the time. Japheth Knopp noted in the Spring 2016 Baseball Research Journal:

> *The manner in which integration in baseball—and in American businesses generally—occurred was not the only model which was possible. It was likely not even the best approach available, but rather served the needs of those in already privileged positions who were able to control not only the manner in which desegregation occurred, but the public perception of it as well in order to exploit the situation for financial gain. Indeed, the very word integration may not be the most applicable in this context because what actually transpired was not so much the fair and equitable combination of two subcultures into one equal and more homogenous group, but rather the reluctant allowance—under certain preconditions—for African Americans to be assimilated into white society.*

To understand the value of a movement, though, is not to understand how it is co-opted by ownership, but to know the people it brings together and what they demand. When Jackie Robinson—the player who demarcated the inevitability of the end of the Negro leagues—attended the March on Washington for Jobs and Freedom in 1963, he did so with his family and marched alongside the people. He stood alongside hundreds of thousands to fight for their common civil and labor rights. "The moral arc of the universe is long," many freedom fighters have echoed, "but it bends towards justice." The bend, it is less frequently said, happens when a great mass of people place the moral arc of the universe on their knee and apply force, as Jackie, his family, and thousands of others did that day.

⚾ ⚾ ⚾

Of course, taking the moral arc of the universe down from the mantle and bending it is not without risk. Perhaps the outsized influence of athletes is itself a mark of a dysfunctional society, but, nonetheless, hundreds of athletes woke up on Wednesday morning with the power to bring in millions of dollars in revenues. That very power, as we would come to find out, was matched with the equal and opposite power to *not* bring those revenues. That power, in hands ranging from the Milwaukee Bucks, to Kenny Smith in the *Inside the NBA* Studio, from the unexpected ally, Josh Hader, and his largely white teammates to the notably Black Seattle Mariners, would be exercised for a single demand: the end to state violence against Black people. Not unlike the March itself, it sat at the intersection of the civil rights of Black Americans and bold labor action. The March on Washington stood in the face of a false notion of integration—against an integration of extraction but not one of equality—and proposed something different. Just the same, the acts of solidarity of August 26, 2020 will be remembered in stark defiance of MLB's BLM-branded, but ultimately empty displays on opening weekend.

Bold defiance like this can never be without risk. By choosing to exercise this power, the Milwaukee Bucks took a risk. They risked vitriol and backlash from those they disagreed with. They risked fines or seeing their contracts voided, as a walkout like this is prohibited by their CBA. They risked forfeiting a playoff game, one that, as the No. 1 seed in the playoffs, they'd worked all year to attain. They didn't know how Orlando would respond. It wasn't clear that other teams throughout the league would follow suit in solidarity. And it wasn't known the league would accept these actions and moderately co-opt them by "postponing" games that would have featured no players.

If the league reschedules the games, some of the athletes' risk—their shared sacrifice—will be diminished, in retrospect. But they did not know any of that when they took that risk. And it is often left to athletes to take these risks when others in society won't, especially those of their same socioeconomic status and levels of influence.

It is athletes, specifically BIPOC athletes, that take them, though, because they live with the risk of being something other than white in this country every day. They are no strangers to the realities of police brutality. It seems incongruous then, to say that sports are a reward for a functioning society when we rely on athletes to lead us closer to being a functioning society. Luckily, our beloved athletes, WNBA players first and foremost among them, understand what sports truly are: a pipebender for the moral arc of the universe.

—Craig Goldstein is editor in chief of Baseball Prospectus. Cory Frontin is an author of Baseball Prospectus.

Index of Names

Allan, Matthew 104, 114
Almora Jr., Albert 94
Alonso, Pete 18
Altherr, Aaron 95
Alvarez, Francisco 96, 115
Aoki, Norichika 96
Barnes, Jacob 50
Baty, Brett 97, 116
Betances, Dellin 52
Brach, Brad 54
Canó, Robinson 20
Carrasco, Carlos 56
Castro, Miguel 58
Céspedes, Yoenis 98
Chirinos, Robinson 22
Conforto, Michael 24
Crow-Armstrong, Pete 98, 115
Davis, J.D. 26
deGrom, Jacob 60
Díaz, Edwin 62
Dominguez, Robert 121
Eickhoff, Jerad 105
Familia, Jeurys 64
Frazier, Todd 28
Ginn, J.T. 105, 117
Greene, Isaiah 118
Gsellman, Robert 66
Guillorme, Luis 99
Heredia, Guillermo 99
Hughes, Jared 68
Hunter, Tommy 70
Jurado, Ariel 106
Kilome, Franklyn 72, 120
Lee, Khalil 100
Lindor, Francisco 30
Loup, Aaron 74
Lucchesi, Joey 76
Lugo, Seth 78
Marisnick, Jake 32
Martínez, José 34
Mauricio, Ronny 101, 113
May, Trevor 80
McCann, James 36
McNeil, Jeff 38
McWilliams, Sam 120
Montgomery, Mike 107
Nido, Tomás 40
Nimmo, Brandon 42
Núñez, Eduardo 101
Oswalt, Corey 82
Palmer, Jaylen 119
Peraza, José 44
Peterson, David 84
Porcello, Rick 86
Ramirez, Alexander 121
Reid-Foley, Sean 88
Rivera, René 102
Smith, Dominic 46
Smith, Mallex 103
Stroman, Marcus 108
Syndergaard, Noah 109
Szapucki, Thomas 110

Tropeano, Nick 111
Valdez, Freddy 120
Vientos, Mark 103, 117
Villar, Jonathan 48
Wilson, Justin 90
Wolf, Josh 118
Yamamoto, Jordan 92

For the Joy of Keeping Score

THIRTY81 Project is an ongoing graphic design project focused on the ballparks of baseball. Since being established in 2013, scorecards have been a fundemental part of the effort. Each two-page card is uniquely ballpark-centric — there are 30 variants — and designed with both beginning and veteran scorekeepers in mind. Evolving over the years with suggestions from fans, broadcasters, and official scorers, the sheets are freely available to everyone as printable letter-size PDFs at the project webshop: www.THIRTY81Project.com

Download, Print, Score, Repeat ...

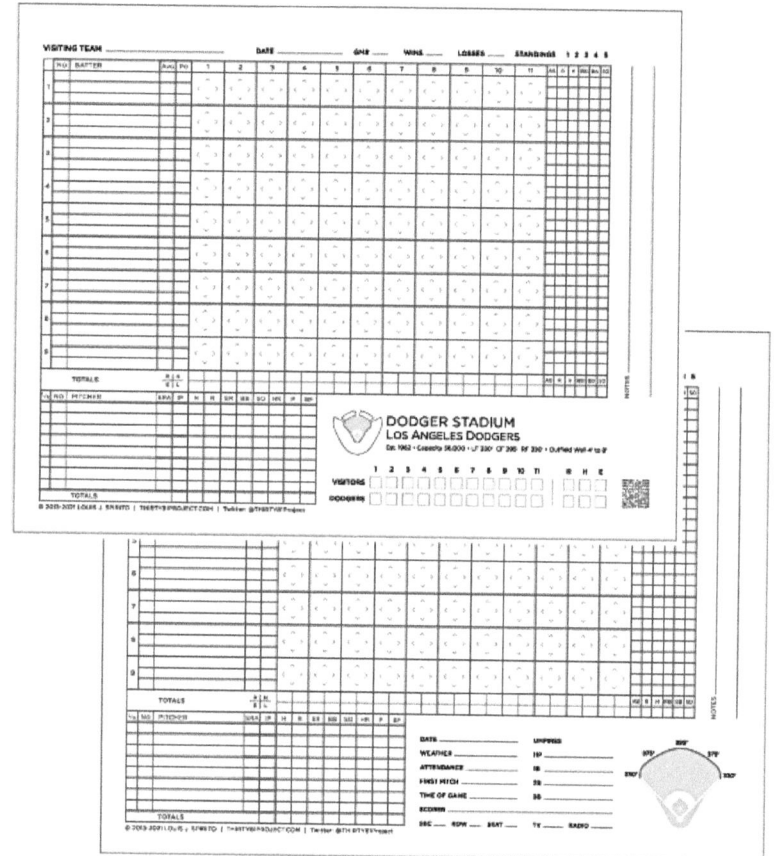

Scorecard design ©2013-2021 Louis J. Spirito | THIRTY81Project